# Libra Shrugged

*Also by David Gerard*

Attack of the 50 Foot Blockchain: Bitcoin, Blockchain, Ethereum
and Smart Contracts

# Libra Shrugged

## How Facebook Tried to Take Over the Money

## David Gerard

First edition, November 2020
ISBN: 9798693053977 (print)

Book site: www.davidgerard.co.uk/blockchain/libra/
Contact the author: dgerard@gmail.com

Art and design: Alli Kirkham www.punkpuns.com/author

1   2   3   4

# Contents

# Introduction: Taking over the money

Facebook was the biggest social network in history. A stupendous, world-shaping success, with around two billion individual users across Facebook, Instagram and WhatsApp.

Facebook and Google overwhelmingly dominated Internet advertising. Facebook made $50 billion from advertising in 2018 — $25 on average for each user, and $112 per North American user.[1]

But no platform is forever. And governments were giving Facebook trouble — over personal data abuses, election rigging and fake news.

A spending spree in the 2010s hadn't helped. Facebook bought Instagram in 2012 for $1 billion, Oculus VR in 2014 for $2 billion, and WhatsApp in 2014 for $19 billion, but these weren't paying off the way Facebook needed them to. Facebook needed an out.

In 2017, Morgan Beller from Facebook's corporate development team had an idea: Facebook could diversify into finance — with something called "blockchain." She sent the idea upwards.

Mark Zuckerberg, Facebook's founder and CEO, looked at Beller's blockchain idea, and wondered: what if Facebook started its own private world currency? Facebook could have so much power that governments couldn't annoy them any more. It would be the Silicon Valley dream.

Facebook announced Libra in June 2019. Libra would be a new global currency and payment system. It would flow instantly around the world by phone. It could even provide financial inclusion for billions: "banking the unbanked." All this, just by using a blockchain.

The details were vague, incomplete and contradictory. The currency would be backed by a reserve — but at some point the Libra "coins" would become completely decentralised and out of anyone's control. Libra would somehow bank the unbanked — but there was no plan for how this would work. Two billion users meant the reserve would be large enough to affect whole countries' financial systems, and knock out small currencies entirely — but nobody involved seemed to have noticed.

But Libra would also make Facebook too big to control — and lead the way for Facebook's Silicon Valley fellows to swing the power of their money as they pleased. Libra would be impossible to regulate; Facebook and their friends could work around any single country's rules.

And Facebook would become the "digital identity" provider to the world. If you wanted to use money at all, you'd have to go through Facebook.

Facebook's plan would also happen to break economies worldwide. Even the US dollar could be shaken. But, trashing entire economies would be a small price for someone else to pay.

Governments looked at Libra, and they saw another 2008 financial crisis in the making. European governments responded within minutes, America within hours, telling Facebook that this couldn't be allowed to happen.

Libra was as incompetent as it was arrogant — and the world stopped it in its tracks.

When Silicon Valley says "disruption," this means they don't understand what they're doing, don't care to understand, and have only contempt for anyone who objects. "Move fast and break things," as Facebook used to put it.

This time, the governments of the world said "no."

But how did Libra fail so hard? How did Facebook spend two years working on Libra, to then put forward such a bizarre and ill-considered plan that left every financial regulator who saw it reeling in horror?

What was Facebook thinking with Libra? And what happens when another company tries the same trick?

Or when Facebook won't take "no" for an answer — and releases the cut-down version that they're already calling "Libra 2.0"?

# Chapter 1:
# A user's guide to Libra

Facebook wants to do its own payment system, called Libra — with its own currency! What does this mean for you? What's the fabulous future that Facebook has planned for you?

None of this exists yet — and it might never exist. In fact, this is the severely cut-down version of what Facebook *really* wanted to do. But if everything does all work out as Facebook has described… it'll work a bit like this.

## What's a Libra? What's it worth?

A Libra is a currency unit in the Libra system. Like dollars, or pounds, or euros. Its symbol is ≈ — three wavy lines.

The exchange rate to your local currency isn't quite fixed — it's set to the average of a "basket" of various other currencies.

If you're buying something where the price isn't listed in Libras, what you pay will go up and down from day to day — welcome to the currency markets! Get used to doing quick calculations whenever you want to buy something.

Or just ignore the Libras, and use your local currency in the Libra system — like you would in PayPal.

## How do I use Libra?

You have a Libra *wallet* — an app on your phone that lets you use your money — probably from Novi (formerly called Calibra), which is Facebook. If you want to use your local currency (dollars, pounds, euros), it'll work a lot like PayPal — you have money in an account on Novi, and you can send money to other Libra users.

If you want to use the Libra currency, you can buy Libras with cash, or sell them for cash. The price will depend on the value of the Libra basket of currencies that day. You'll need to have your government identification on file with Novi.

You can send money or Libras to anyone with a Libra wallet — Novi or not — anywhere in the world.

You can buy things with Libras — if they're for sale with a price in Libras.

## What about my personal information? This is pretty private stuff.

Novi says that it won't share your data with the main Facebook organisation — except in as-yet-undefined circumstances.

Kevin Weil, vice president of product for Novi, says: "Your financial data will never be used to target ads on Facebook."[2]

You can definitely trust Facebook on this firm promise! And never mind all the times Facebook broke privacy promises previously, including their 2019 Federal Trade Commission fine and settlement for breaking their previous 2011 settlement over privacy issues.

Libra looks very like Facebook building a massive data-miner on top of the entire system of consumer commerce — but they told US Congress that this definitely won't happen with Novi, at least. It'll be fine.

## Am I stuck with Facebook and Novi?

There will apparently be other Libra wallet providers — though as of late 2020, no-one else has announced any plans. Facebook apps, such as Messenger and WhatsApp, will only be able to use Novi — but you'll be able to send Libras (or dollars or pounds or euros on Libra) to and from the other providers, if any ever come along.

Novi promises full data portability — so you can move all your Libra money and data to a new provider.[3]

## So I can send money to anyone?

Almost anyone! You have to keep to the anti-money-laundering laws you're under right now.

Sometimes people will send you money or Libras, and Novi will freeze the payment. Or you'll try to send money or Libras, and you'll be told Novi can't let you pay that person. Or sometimes Novi will freeze your account, or suddenly shut it down.

This is just like PayPal does, for the same reasons — which they may or may not tell you. All of this follows directly from the anti-money-laundering laws — so Novi can't legally promise you that none of this will ever happen.

But Novi-to-Novi transfers will *almost certainly* go through!

# Is this a cryptocurrency? Can I get rich from this?

Libra is based on cryptocurrency ideas, but it all revolves around "stablecoins" — digital currencies that try to keep a fixed value. The Libra currency unit is not intended to be an investment or a speculative gamble, like buying bitcoins and hoping they'll go up in price, or foreign exchange trading. (It might turn out to be one in practice.)

The ordinary currencies on Libra will always be exchangeable at $1 on Libra = $1 cash, £1 on Libra =£1 cash, and so on. The price of the Libra currency itself is calculated from the national currencies to be as stable as possible, even if they change price against each other.

# What's a cryptocurrency, anyway? Do I care?

Probably not. From your perspective, the stuff on Libra is money, and you can spend it on things — the same way you can spend Amazon gift voucher dollars, or loyalty points at supermarkets.

Novi says they'll keep track of things for you — they're doing a "custodial wallet," which would work a lot like having money in an account at PayPal. Novi will have customer support if you lose your phone or your password, or if you get scammed.[4]

This isn't the usual case with cryptocurrencies. With Bitcoin and so on, if someone picks your pocket from the other side of the world, those are their coins now — getting your coins back is tedious and unlikely.

You can use a different custodial wallet for your money on Libra, which will be under much the same rules as Novi.

Some crypto[*] fans like to live dangerously and keep the cryptographic keys to their crypto-coins themselves, like keeping your savings in a sock under your mattress — all the control, all the risk, and they might have trouble sending money on Libra to or from the

---

[*] Cryptographers get understandably annoyed when "cryptocurrency" is shortened to "crypto." Sadly, it's standard finance jargon now.

Novi system — but the financial regulators absolutely won't be letting that happen with Libra in the foreseeable future.

## How does any of this make my life better? Why should I sign up?

Libra promises a fabulously efficient financial future — "paying bills with the push of a button, buying a cup of coffee with the scan of a code or riding your local public transit without needing to carry cash or a metro pass."[5] Imagine if you could do all of that!

If you're in Europe or Asia rather than the United States, you've had all of that for the past decade or so with the card or phone that's already in your pocket — without a weird "basket" currency in the way.

A lot of the problems that Facebook claims Libra solves are really just US retail banking being a few decades behind the rest of the world — sending money between banks can take days, everything has fees, so many things need a phone call, paper checks are still a thing, and so on. But it's standard in Silicon Valley to propose an all-encompassing international system, and base it entirely on looking out your window in Palo Alto.

Various commentators have come up with ideas on how Facebook could make Libra more tempting as a product — promotions, discounts and so on — but none of these have been suggested by Facebook itself.

The important use cases that Facebook and Libra have put forward are sending money internationally, and giving access to finance to billions of people who don't have it yet — "banking the unbanked." They've also suggested that more commerce in general will mean Facebook might be able to sell ads for higher prices. They're not at all clear on the tricky details for any of these.

In the meantime, Libra will be a sort of PayPal, but on Facebook. Maybe that'll be useful to you.

## What's the point of all this?

There's the obvious motivation where Facebook gets to see all your spending data. But why are they doing it like this? Why's there a new currency in there? Why's there a "blockchain?"

This PayPal-but-it's-Facebook system is Libra's fallback position from what they originally wanted to build — which was a much weirder system, based on some wild ideas they got from Bitcoin and the other cryptocurrencies.

None of these ideas would work at scale, and everything would break. This is what got governments around the world so upset at Libra, so quickly.

So why did anyone think this was a good idea?

# Chapter 2:
# The genesis of Libra:
# Beller's blockchain

One day in mid-2017, Morgan Beller, who had recently joined Facebook's corporate development team, proposed to her supervisor that she start looking into how Facebook could get into blockchains and cryptocurrencies.

Beller had worked on Andreessen Horowitz's cryptocurrency venture capital fund. She was increasingly sure that a "seismic" shift was coming to finance.[6] The price of Bitcoin was rising dizzily at the time — around $3,000 a bitcoin, up from just $750 in January — and "blockchain" was the hot buzzword.

Beller went out into the blockchain world, met with cryptocurrency people, and asked venture capitalists questions like: "If you had a platform of over two billion users, how would you go about trying to integrate blockchain technology into the platform?"[7]

Morgan Beller had grown up on Long Island, the daughter of corporate operations executive and consultant Michael Beller. She studied at Cornell University from 2010 to 2013, graduating with a Bachelor of Science degree in statistical informatics.

At Cornell, Beller was part of the Alpha Kappa Psi business fraternity. She co-founded the PopShop, a collaborative space for student entrepreneurs. She credits her "passion for venture capital" to her experience volunteering at TechCrunch Disrupt in 2011 — "That was my first exposure to the tech world, and I became completely intoxicated."[8]

After Cornell, Beller worked at eBay for three months as a product manager, then joined venture capital firm Andreessen Horowitz ("a16z"), getting involved in Andreessen's cryptocurrency fund — which got her interested in the Bitcoin and blockchain world. "Crypto is a mental virus for which there is no cure. I was at a16z when they got infected with the crypto virus."[9]

Beller joined blogging platform Medium in April 2016, in strategy and corporate development. She moved to Facebook in May 2017, where she started working on blockchains.

Beller wrote a memo to persuade Facebook executives that they had an opportunity to be leaders on this new platform — or risk being disrupted by it. She won over David Marcus, the Vice President of Messaging Products (Facebook Messenger) — who happened to be an early Bitcoin fan.

Marcus takes credit for the idea of Facebook doing its own cryptocurrency: "I'm guilty," he told reporters in October 2019.[10] Marcus had been thinking about something like Libra for several years.

David Marcus was born in France in 1973 and grew up in Geneva in Switzerland.[11] He studied economics at the University of Geneva, before dropping out to work at a bank to support his family.[12] But he really wanted to go into business for himself. He founded his first company, GTN Telecom, in 1996.

His mobile phone payments company Zong was bought by PayPal, which was then owned by eBay, in 2011. John Donahoe, CEO of eBay, made Marcus the president of PayPal in March 2012 — for his "founder's perspective" and "start-up energy."[13]

Marcus revamped PayPal's engineering team, and oversaw acquisitions such as Venmo. He sent out memos calling for more enthusiasm for the company's products — "It's been brought to my attention that when testing paying with mobile at Cafe 17 last week, some of you refused to install the PayPal app (!!?!?!!), and others didn't even remember their PayPal password" — and noting how "employees in other offices hack into Coke machines to make them accept PayPal because they feel passionately about using PayPal everywhere. I don't see these behaviors here in San Jose."[14]

In late 2012, Argentina ordered PayPal to cut off direct payments between Argentinians. Marcus saw the price of Bitcoin rise as the new rule went into effect — and he wondered if Argentinians were buying bitcoins instead. He set up an account at Mt. Gox, the biggest Bitcoin exchange at the time, and started buying bitcoins himself.[15]

By March 2013, Marcus had set up a group inside PayPal to see how the company might harness Bitcoin or blockchains — though Bitcoin's price volatility, and worries about regulation, made PayPal think that adding Bitcoin wasn't a great idea yet. PayPal did continue to consider integrating Bitcoin into its products.

Marcus also attended the Bitcoin Foundation's first conference, in May 2013 — though he turned his name badge around, so that people wouldn't realise the president of PayPal was there. He was appalled by the naïveté of the Bitcoin companies, and their lack of understanding of money-laundering laws and basic compliance issues.

Marcus met with Mark Zuckerberg of Facebook for dinner in 2014, expecting to discuss a business deal with PayPal — and was surprised to be offered a job at Facebook, running Messenger. He started at Facebook soon after. He wrote on LinkedIn at the time, "I realized that my role was becoming a real management one, vs. my passion of building products that hopefully matter to a lot of people."[16]

Marcus brought the cryptocurrency idea to Zuckerberg in late 2017, and they talked about their frustrations with present-day payment systems. Both Marcus and Zuckerberg thought a blockchain-based cryptocurrency might let Facebook work around banking system middlemen — and the fees and delays involved in the regulated environment.

Marcus felt that PayPal had capitulated to regulators. With a cryptocurrency, Facebook could realise the libertarian dream of pure and borderless Internet money — freed from fragmented rules and markets.[17]

Zuckerberg started reading up on blockchains and cryptocurrencies. In his "personal challenges" blog post of 4 January 2018, he wrote:[18]

> There are important counter-trends to this — like encryption and cryptocurrency — that take power from centralized systems and put it back into people's hands. But they come with the risk of being harder to control. I'm interested to go deeper and study the positive and negative aspects of these technologies, and how best to use them in our services.

On 8 May 2018, Marcus announced that he was leaving Facebook Messenger to lead a team dedicated to "exploring blockchain technology"[19] [20] — and to put some executive muscle behind Beller's ideas.

# Chapter 3:
# To launch a Libra:
# Let's start a crypto

On 11 May 2018, news site Cheddar revealed that Facebook's blockchain group was looking into a cryptocurrency for the company's billions of users. "'They are very serious about it,' said one of the people, who asked not to be identified discussing unannounced plans." This was the first public news that Facebook was planning a cryptocurrency.[21]

Around the end of 2018, the Facebook blockchain unit even suggested using the Facebook cryptocurrency for money transfer on WhatsApp in India.[22]

(Indian regulators demanded that all personal data be held locally, and not sent back to California for processing — which Facebook didn't agree to until August 2019,[23] The version of WhatsApp Pay that finally went live in India was a front-end to India's Unified Payments Interface — just like Google Pay in India — and just used rupees.)

The blockchain unit started hiring more staff — especially researchers, cryptographers and academics. Marcus also took on ex-PayPal executives.[24] The unit had 32 staff by the beginning of 2019. Morale was slipping — they weren't sure if the project would ever go live. But Mark Zuckerberg finally gave the green light in January.[25]

By February 2019, Facebook was talking to cryptocurrency exchanges about selling their new crypto-coin — which would not float in value like Bitcoin, but would instead be a "stablecoin," its value pegged to a basket of conventional currencies.[26]

## Collecting friends

The blockchain unit considered that Facebook shouldn't try to do a new currency on its own. They started looking for partners for the project, to form a Libra Association.

Companies needed to be of a particular minimum size (*e.g.*, $1 billion in market value, or a reach of greater than 20 million users), and nonprofits needed a five-year track record. If you wanted to run a processing node on the Libra blockchain network, you'd need to put up $10 million — though, contrary to early reports, nobody had to put in the $10 million at the time of the public announcement.[27]

Facebook didn't look very far to find Libra Association members. Most were closely associated with David Marcus and Facebook — they shared board members with Facebook, had significant investors in common, or employed former Facebook executives. One academic called it "a club run by like-minded, interconnected elites interested in power and profit." Another called it "a façade of decentralisation," and thought it likely the members would collude.[28] [29]

Facebook promised partners that it would relinquish control of Libra once it was up and running.[25] Venture capitalists Andreessen Horowitz, Morgan Beller's previous employers, were quite clear that Libra would not just be Facebook's show: "One of the key factors in our decision to join was that we would in fact have — and all members would have — an equal vote," said general partner Kathryn Haun.[30]

## News gets out

The blockchain unit was trying hard to keep its work confidential, even from the rest of Facebook — but details were leaking all over the press, as Facebook staff met with potential partners in the venture. David Marcus decided that they would launch the project — even though neither their plan nor their software were fully worked out as yet.

The internal code name in 2019 was "Libra." Facebook decided they wanted this to be the production name — so, on 20 April, Facebook bought the US trademark for "Libra" from an existing company, Libra Services, Inc., who made tax and accounting software for cryptocurrency companies. (That company changed its name to "Lukka."[31])

On 2 May 2019, Facebook registered Libra Networks in Switzerland, "to provide financial and technology services and develop related hardware and software." This was the first public use of the name.

On the same day, the Wall Street Journal reported that Facebook's year-old cryptocurrency project was called Libra, and that they were "recruiting dozens of financial firms and online merchants" for investments of about $1 billion to serve as the backing reserve that would stabilise the currency — though Facebook wouldn't comment, saying only that they were "exploring many different applications."[32]

# Surely not a cryptocurrency?

Nobody could understand why Facebook would do their new payment system as a blockchain. A free-floating cryptocurrency would go up and down in value compared to the user's own currency — normal people wouldn't put up with "money" that was going up and down all the time.

A "permissioned" blockchain — where someone runs it and controls who can use it — is just a slow distributed database. Companies only do these so they can use the buzzword "blockchain" in their press release.

A "permissionless" cryptocurrency like Bitcoin is built to be out of anyone's control, wastes incredible amounts of electricity — Bitcoin uses about as much power as all of Austria[43] — and would be a completely silly idea for a company to develop as an investment, unless they were maintaining control by other means.

Money transmission has very strict regulation — and Bitcoin and its many descendants were created specifically to work around government rules.

There was a plausible business in payments — something like PayPal, but run by Facebook — because this had worked really well for the WeChat messaging network in China. This would even give Facebook large amounts of data on its users' spending habits, so they could sell even more finely targeted advertising.

In fact, Facebook already had a payments system — Messenger Payments, which had been running in the US since 2015.

What would a cryptocurrency let a regulated company do that a company like PayPal didn't do already? Nothing that anyone could think of.

# The Libra Association assembles

By the June 2019 announcement, Facebook had gathered twenty-seven other companies to the Libra Association.

Facebook asked some of the partner companies to co-sign the Libra white papers that Facebook had written — though many of them weren't yet clear on how the coin would work, or what their roles would be.[33]

No cryptocurrency news sites were invited to the pre-launch press conferences — so instead, via multiple helpful leakers, crypto site The Block was first in the world to publish the full list of Libra

Association members, on Saturday 15 June.[34] The Block also got a copy of Libra's official announcement, due to go out the following Tuesday.

The initial partners were:

- **Payments:** Mastercard, Mercado Pago, PayPal, PayU, Stripe, Visa
- **Technology and marketplaces:** Booking Holdings (booking.com, Priceline), eBay, Calibra (Facebook), Farfetch (fashion), Lyft (minicabs), Spotify (music), Uber (minicabs)
- **Telecommunications:** Iliad, Vodafone Group
- **Blockchain:** Anchorage (crypto-asset custody), BisonTrails (blockchain platform), Coinbase (cryptocurrency exchange), Xapo (crypto-asset custody)
- **Venture capital:** Andreessen Horowitz, Breakthrough Initiatives, Creative Destruction Lab, Ribbit Capital, Thrive Capital, Union Square Ventures
- **Nonprofit:** Kiva, Mercy Corps, Women's World Banking

Apart from payment companies, every member of note was a blockchain company, a venture capital firm, a company running at a loss to acquire customers, or a nonprofit.

The absences were noteworthy — no Apple Pay, no Google Pay, no Amazon, no Microsoft … and no banks.

David Marcus told the Financial Times that he wanted to "absolutely and strongly deny the fact that we've approached banks and banks have said no." Banks said otherwise — ING confirmed to the paper that they had rejected an approach to join.

Facebook had also approached Goldman Sachs, JP Morgan Chase and Fidelity Investments, all of whom declined — even as Fidelity had been getting into crypto. "The challenge with cryptocurrencies is the opaqueness as to the sources of the money," said Mike Corbat of Citigroup, even as he called himself a "true believer" in cryptocurrencies.

Bank executives who had been approached by Facebook worried about regulation and practicality — "We see hurdles to scale, we see hurdles to adoption, we see enough of this to decide that we would not participate in a scheme like this."[35]

One banker said Facebook's fundamental error had been to announce their plan without bringing regulators onside first of all — which no sensible financial institution would have done.[36] If Libra didn't fully address regulators' fears on money-laundering, banks might have had to drop Facebook itself as a customer. (Unbanking the banked.)[37]

PayPal had only been approached a few weeks before the Libra announcement. The PayPal[38] and Visa[39] press releases both spoke very positively about Libra, but conspicuously failed to commit to any specific actions.

Mastercard, one of the last companies to sign up, said later that the $10 million ante was smaller than some of their sponsorship deals.[40] Their press statement didn't even use the word "Libra." Other members declined to send out a press release or speak to the media about Libra.

Several companies told the New York Times in June that they only signed up because they weren't obliged to do anything — to promote Libra, to use Libra or to pay money into the Association — and could back out later. They were already hesitant to get too close to Facebook and its controversies — and how it had mistreated its partners in the past.[41]

## The announcement

Facebook unveiled Libra in an embargoed press preview at the old San Francisco Mint building on 11 June 2019. Select members of the UK press were invited to a further press conference on Saturday 15 June.

Journalists at the Saturday press conference asked directly why Facebook's project used a cryptocurrency — what that got them over not doing it as a cryptocurrency — and couldn't get a sensible answer.

David Marcus held a further press conference on Monday 17 June. He told how Mark Zuckerberg was interested in the project and the ideas — "A high quality medium of exchange for the world, on a blockchain that could scale."

The big moment was Tuesday 18 June at 07:00 UTC — at midnight in California, 3AM in New York and 8AM in London, the full documents were put up on the *libra.org* website, newspapers released their analyses, and the world dived into the details.

Within hours of Facebook's announcement, governments and financial regulators worldwide were calling for Libra to be halted immediately.

# Chapter 4:
# Bitcoin: why Libra is like this

In truth, the gold standard is already a barbarous relic.

— John Maynard Keynes[42]

Libra is an attempt by Facebook to set up a private currency. But a huge amount of the fuss around Libra was that it would be a "blockchain" or a "cryptocurrency." Like that "Bitcoin" thing that was big a few years ago. Business revolution, and magical free Internet money, maybe!

Libra's connection to blockchains is partly the technology — but it's mostly the ideas. Libra lifts heavily from Bitcoin. Everyone involved was a massive Bitcoin fan.

Every question Bitcoin and blockchain ask is a human problem — and the standard tech company answer is to use computer programs to do an end-run around the human element. (And especially around the regulatory element.) This always ends as badly as you'd expect — and that's how Libra crashed and burned.

So — what's a blockchain, anyway?

## What is a blockchain?

Technically, a blockchain is simple. It's an append-only ledger (using a data structure called a *Merkle tree*) — like an account book where you can only add new entries, not alter or remove old ones — and some mechanism to decide who adds the next entry. You can distribute copies of the ledger, and anyone receiving one can check they have a good copy.

That's it. That's the whole thing.* Blockchains are *really simple* — and when normal people find out what a blockchain actually is, they go: "What? That's not magical at all. How do they get all of the nonsense I've read out of that?"

---

\* There are systems that are marketed as "blockchain" and claim all sorts of near-magical properties of blockchains — but might have just the append-only ledger, or not even that. Or systems that claim the magic of "blockchain," but just use a blockchain-like system as a back-end data store — most IBM press releases about "blockchain" are like this. But "append-only ledger with a consensus mechanism" is a reasonable working definition.

The weird hype and apocalyptic claims come from Bitcoin — the digital money that was the 2008 origin of the blockchain as we know it.

## Digital cash

Digital cash is an obviously useful idea — something that works like notes and coins, but you can pass it around by computer, and over the Internet.

A common way to do this now is that you have a card — or maybe an app on your phone — that's attached to your bank account. Wave the card or phone, you've bought your morning coffee.

So who gets to process transactions, and make sure that nobody spends their money twice? The solution the world has mostly come to is to use a system run by banks and money transmitters — centralised entities, heavily regulated by law.

But this wasn't good enough for the people who became Bitcoin fans — they wanted a payment system with no central controller at all.

## How Bitcoin works

Bitcoin was invented in 2008 by a programmer calling himself Satoshi Nakamoto. He described Bitcoin as a payment system — "electronic peer-to-peer cash."

Bitcoin has a public blockchain. Anyone can look at it. The Bitcoin blockchain includes every Bitcoin transaction since Bitcoin was launched in January 2009.

When you "have" a Bitcoin, you have the key to a particular Bitcoin address on the public Bitcoin blockchain — like a password. If you lose the key, you've lost your coins. Other cryptocurrencies work the same way.

The problem was: how to add new transactions to the ledger, without a central controller who could be told what to do by a government. Governments were the original threat model for Bitcoin.

What Bitcoin does is run a computerised lottery, in a process called "mining." Bitcoin miners guess a number. They take their guess, they combine it with a block of transactions that are waiting to be processed, and they do a simple calculation on them. If the calculation gives a small enough number, the miner wins six-and-a-quarter fresh new bitcoins! And their block of transactions is added to the public blockchain.

The more guesses you make, the better your chances. In June 2020, Bitcoin miners were making 100 quintillion guesses every second. This used as much electricity as all of Austria.[43] This is called "proof-of-work" — though it might better be termed "proof-of-waste."

Blocks come out approximately every ten minutes. If miners win coins too often, the difficulty goes up, to slow the system down — so the miners have to add more computers to compete. This results in spiraling electricity use — Bitcoin is, literally, anti-efficient.

The point of all this waste is to secure the blockchain — the threat model is that nobody can change the blockchain without wasting at least as much electricity.

The Bitcoin mining system is incredibly slow, and very hard to scale up. Bitcoin now consumes between 0.1% and 0.5% of all the electricity in the world — for the same seven transactions per second, worldwide, that it could do in 2009, when it was just running on Nakamoto's desktop PC. Bitcoin is the most inefficient payment network in human history.

Bitcoin filled its tiny transaction capacity and clogged in mid-2015 — making transactions slow, unreliable and expensive ever since. As a payment system, Bitcoin can only work as a toy proof-of-concept.

So why did anyone think this was a good idea?

## The Bitcoin ideology

Bitcoin wasn't really created to be a new payment system. Bitcoin was a political project to make money that worked in a certain way — to enforce a particular ideology.

Bitcoin is based on ideas from a particular subculture of cryptographers, the "cypherpunks" of the 1990s, who were into the "anarcho-capitalism" of heterodox American economist Murray Rothbard and the Austrian School of economics.[44]

The key concept is extremist libertarianism. Not just less regulation, and more freedoms for business — but *no* regulations, and *total* freedom for business. Somehow, complicated social property rights would still exist without any government.

The cypherpunks wouldn't tolerate even the possibility of governments interfering in their money — or being able to reach into their bank accounts. So Nakamoto used an append-only Merkle tree ledger to make transactions irreversible. No authority could take your coins without the cryptographic key to those coins — or stop you sending your coins anywhere you liked.

The original purpose of cryptocurrency was to evade all government control or regulation. This was the key design constraint.

Bitcoin had a limited supply, like a gold standard — you can't just "print money." Bitcoin's advocates also didn't like credit, which was a major cause of the financial crisis of 2008 — they thought the actual digital "gold" itself should always be used as money. This would enforce financial discipline. (Of course, people started lending bitcoins and extending credit as soon as this became a thing you could do.)

"Gold standard" is a common phrase meaning that something is good and trustworthy — but the actual gold standard, which started in the 1790s, didn't work well at all. Gold standard economies went through manic boom-and-bust cycles and financial crises. Countries came out of the Great Depression of the 1930s as they moved off a rigid gold standard, and the last traces of the gold standard were abandoned in 1971. Real economies need credit and monetary policy for any sort of stability. Bitcoiners think that this is incorrect and immoral, and that bad ideas that didn't work before will surely work again if they're programmed well enough.

Of course, the most common pitch for Bitcoin is much simpler: you might get rich for free. People will say and do any ridiculous thing if they might get rich for free. The one really consistent ideology in Bitcoin is: "number go up."

## The fabulous promises of Bitcoin!

The first bitcoiners tended to be quite clever in the manner of engineers — what they didn't understand about economics, they were confident would just be a simple matter of programming. Actual bankers and mainstream economists said Bitcoin ideas were completely wrong and silly — so obviously those must have been fake disciplines.

Bitcoin became a study in how to reinvent the entire financial system from scratch — badly.

Bitcoin comes with a string of promises. It's totally decentralised! You don't have to trust anyone, so it's immune to bad actors! Bitcoin will get rid of middlemen! Money can flow instantly and internationally, for free!

Bitcoin doesn't realise any of these in practice, but the fans are still sure it does, or will, or could. As long as the price might go up.

Decentralised systems always tend to centralise, because that's more cost-effective. Bitcoin mining has economies of scale — so by early 2014, it had centralised. By July 2014, one entity controlled over 50% of all bitcoin mining. By 2015, the controllers of 90% of Bitcoin mining stood together on a single conference stage.[45]

Bitcoin is famously plagued by scams — because transactions are irreversible. All frauds, hacks, and fat-finger fumbles are final. If I pick your pocket from the other side of the world, those are my bitcoins now.

Bitcoin wasn't used much until you could reliably exchange it for actual money, in early 2011. This led to an elaborate structure of middlemen — like the existing world of finance, but incompetent. You can access the Bitcoin blockchain directly — but in practice, almost everyone keeps their bitcoins on an exchange.

Bitcoin's uncensorability made it a favourite for criminals. The first real use case for Bitcoin was the Silk Road darknet drug market. Bitcoiners questioned whether this was even a crime, morally speaking — though the authorities didn't see it that way. It turned out that registering your crimes on a permanent public ledger of all transactions wasn't a good idea.

Transactions on the Bitcoin blockchain clogged in mid-2015, and have been slow and expensive since. Transaction fees peaked at an average of around $55 in December 2017.

There are various proposed "layer two" fixes for the Bitcoin transaction clog that do the real work off to the side somewhere. The most loudly advocated is the Lightning Network — which doesn't scale either, and whose toy implementation has already centralised.[46]

Censorship resistance just isn't a problem ordinary people have in day-to-day life. They want convenience and reliability — and the Bitcoin system is absolutely not convenient or reliable as a payment system.

The Bitcoin promises are still out there, and they're used to try to get people to buy bitcoins — so the big holders can finally cash out. The promises are also used to promote other Bitcoin-like cryptocurrencies. They're even used to promote completely centralised uses — such as initial coin offering (ICO) tokens, where a central controlling entity makes a pile of digital tokens and sells them. Bitcoin promises are even used to promote private non-currency enterprise blockchains.

Prospective users hear the blockchain hype and assume the hypothetical plans are real products that exist now — though "the blockchain could" is a phrase that really means "the blockchain doesn't," because if it did, they'd say that.

Libra got a bit of publicity on these promises — though Facebook understood they'd have to deliver something that worked much better as a currency.

## Other cryptocurrencies

Once Bitcoin existed, it could be copied — and so, from about mid-2011, people started making their *own* magical Internet money. There were thousands of variants in short order. These were generically called "cryptocurrencies," or "cryptos."

Some tried new ideas. Ethereum adds "smart contracts," which are small computer programs that run right there on the blockchain; if Bitcoin is like an Excel spreadsheet, Ethereum is like a spreadsheet with macros. And the Ethereum subculture isn't as ideological. New cryptocurrencies tend to include smart contract functionality, and so Libra does too.

Ripple Labs' XRP is a cryptocurrency without the hideous electricity waste of mining — though it's ultimately controlled by Ripple, through some obfuscation. ICO tokens are completely centrally-controlled objects — though they'll often be marketed as "decentralised" anyway.

All these different kinds of token are called "cryptos," and they all trade on the same exchanges as Bitcoin. They all trade freely against each other and ordinary currencies, and their prices can go up and down wildly.

## Why didn't Libra just use Bitcoin?

David Marcus had long understood Bitcoin's problems as a currency — mainly that the price of a bitcoin wasn't stable, and could go up or down 10% in a day. He said in 2013:[47]

> It's a great place to put assets, especially in places like Argentina with forty per cent inflation, where one dollar today is worth sixty cents in a year, and a government's currency does not hold value. It's also a good investment vehicle if you have an appetite for risk. But it won't be a currency until volatility slows down.

Marcus knew that Libra's value had to be stable. He explained to CNBC in October 2019 why Libra wouldn't just use Bitcoin:[48]

> If there was a stable, low-volatility, scalable version of Bitcoin that we could use today, my life would be so

much simpler. We could just focus on embedding that in the Calibra wallet.

But one trick Libra could take from Bitcoin's gold-standard thinking was to make the "coins" strictly represent a reserve — the actual value, stored away in a reserve somewhere.

## Libra as a stablecoin

In cryptocurrency trading, a *stablecoin* is a crypto that is kept at a more-or-less steady value — and won't go up and down like Bitcoin. Stablecoins are the crypto equivalent of regulated electronic money (e-money).

The largest stablecoin is Tether, which claims that each tether is backed one-to-one by a US dollar in a bank account — or perhaps by loans, or by bitcoins, or maybe by hot air; Tether is under investigation by the New York Attorney General over the integrity of their reserve, and questions as to just what they're backing these tethers with.[49]

Tethers are popular in crypto trading because they're "dollars" that move around the world at the speed of crypto. Much faster than moving actual money around — with all those tedious money-laundering rules. For a while, Tether openly touted evading regulation as its advantage.[50] When a crypto trader says "stablecoin," they mean something like Tether.

Tether's backing reserve has never been audited — does it even exist? — and there are no verified cases of anyone cashing out their tethers for dollars. So other stablecoins came along — more regulated, with audits and so on. These were for the crypto trading market — they weren't e-money for consumers to use.

Libra's currency could have just represented a single national currency in this way, like dollars or euros — but Facebook wanted the coin to work around the world. So the Libra currency would be based on the average value of a "basket" of several national currencies — in the hope that would make it mostly-stable compared to any one national currency.

This is not quite the same sort of thing as Tether. But outside crypto, the term "stablecoin" now means "Libra" — when a bank, financial regulator or government says "stablecoin," it's always a euphemism for Libra.

So, Libra was inspired by Bitcoin and other cryptocurrencies. But how could Libra make a version of these ideas work for ordinary end users?

# Chapter 5:
# The Libra White Papers

One of the great mistakes is to judge policies and
programs by their intentions rather than their results.

— Milton Friedman[51]

Libra started in blockchain dreams. Libra's creators wanted
something that would give them what Bitcoin had promised.

The Libra team wanted Bitcoin, but without Bitcoin's technical
problems, and run by *sensible* people — *i.e.*, themselves.

The Libra white papers are the plan that Facebook's blockchain
unit wrote up and presented to the world, including the regulators. In
many cases, this was all they presented to the regulators.

## The white papers go live

For many years, the web address *libra.org* had served a short page
about the Libra star sign.[52] This was replaced some time in November
2018 with a blank page.

At 07:00 UTC on 18 June 2019, a new page, "Libra: A New
Global Currency" appeared[53] — urging you to "Read the White
Paper."

In the cryptocurrency world, a "white paper" is a sort of
investment prospectus — telling how the promoters' made-up private
money for bananas[54] or dentistry[55] will revolutionise the world
economy, and achieve trillions of dollars in total supply. And
probably bank the unbanked.

Keeping to this tradition, Facebook released a series of white
papers for the June 2019 announcement of Libra. There were
multiple quiet updates to the various white papers after the US Senate
and House hearings in July — but we'll talk here about the original
release versions, finalised between 14 and 17 June 2019. These were
what financial regulators, central bankers and journalists were reading
closely in the days and weeks following the announcement.[56]

The main Libra white paper was full of half-explained new ideas,
which puzzled a lot of ordinary readers. But those who'd followed
the cryptocurrency world found the concepts eerily familiar — they

were claims that Bitcoin fans had made over the years, to try to get people to buy bitcoins.

## Libra's mission: bank the world

We start with the mission statement:

> Libra's mission is to enable a simple global currency and financial infrastructure that empowers billions of people.

Billions of people around the world have cheap smartphones and a connection to the Internet. This has helped access to the financial system — but 1.7 billion people remain excluded, even though, of that 1.7 billion, "one billion have a mobile phone and nearly half a billion have internet access."

The white paper states the problem, then says that blockchains can "potentially" address the causes — "this approach can deliver a giant leap forward toward a lower-cost, more accessible, and more connected global financial system."

Sounds great! How will it do that? The white paper never quite answers this question — it just says, over and over, that a blockchain system will definitely do this:

> … the software that implements the Libra Blockchain is open source — designed so that anyone can build on it, and billions of people can depend on it for their financial needs. Imagine an open, interoperable ecosystem of financial services that developers and organizations will build to help people and businesses hold and transfer Libra for everyday use.

Other parts of the Libra plan had secondary white papers, explaining their ideas in detail — but financial inclusion, the key promise and mission of Libra, did not.

## The Libra Association

Facebook formed the Libra Association to issue and govern the Libra coin, and recruited twenty-seven other companies to become members of the Association — payment providers, a few nonprofits, and a pile of companies from the worlds of cryptocurrency, Silicon Valley venture capital, or both.

The Association would choose who could run processing nodes for the Libra blockchain. It would choose new members for the

Association; Facebook hoped to get to one hundred Association members in due course.

It would also create Libra tokens — the digital "coins" of the currency itself — when a Libra reseller gave the Association money to put into the backing reserve, and it would destroy the tokens when a reseller cashed coins out.

The Association would supervise the development of the Libra blockchain software. This included developing an "open identity standard" — though these initial white papers had no detail on Libra's plans for this either, just a single sentence in the main white paper: "We believe that decentralized and portable digital identity is a prerequisite to financial inclusion and competition."

Organisations trying to bank the unbanked have long thought that a robust digital identity of some sort might help people without paperwork into the financial system. And Facebook, of course, has long collected as much data as it can on individuals, to target advertising. Though as of 2020, there doesn't appear to have been any technical work on an identity system for Libra.

Facebook was a member of the Association via their Calibra unit (now called Novi). In fact, at this time, Facebook was the only member of the Association — everyone else was just a prospective member. Facebook stressed that they were just one member of many — though if twenty-seven mice are in bed with an elephant, they probably can't stop the elephant from rolling over.[57]

## The Libra Reserve

The Libra currency tokens would be backed by a reserve, managed by the Libra Association.

End users wouldn't have direct access to the reserve — you'd convert your Libras to and from actual money at an authorised reseller, such as Facebook's Calibra, or maybe at a cryptocurrency exchange.

A Libra token would not be backed by a single currency — but by a *basket* of currencies, with the price of a Libra token being a weighted average of its component currencies. The white papers didn't list the makeup of the basket, but as of September 2019, the component currencies were going to be the US dollar, the Euro, the Japanese yen, the British pound sterling and the Singapore dollar.[58] So the value of one Libra token would be variable — but hopefully not too variable.

The reserve would be filled by end users buying Libra tokens for cash, before they gave them to someone else, who would sell them for cash. As such, the reserve would be the working float in the Libra payment system.

The secondary white paper "The Libra Reserve" goes into more detail.[59] The reserve would be "a collection of low-volatility assets, including bank deposits and government securities in currencies from stable and reputable central banks." The Libra system would be seeded with coins provided by the Association to its members, and those coins would be paid for by "a private placement to investors."[*]

The interest on the reserve would pay for running costs, offset transaction fees ... and pay dividends to the companies who had bought Libra Investment Tokens to fund the Libra Association. (The Libra Investment Token idea was quietly scrubbed from all the Libra white papers in July 2019, and never mentioned again.)

The link between Libra currency tokens and the backing reserve would only be a promise by the Libra Association — they'd issue Libra tokens as liabilities against the reserve. This is not quite the same as your bank deposits being liabilities that the bank owes to you — only the Libra resellers could redeem the liability represented by the Libra token. If you wanted cash for your Libra tokens, you could only take them to a reseller. If the Libra reserve went broke, the resellers would be out of luck, so you'd be out of luck.

# The magic of blockchain

Blockchains sound pretty cool and awesome in the white paper:

> Blockchains and cryptocurrencies have a number of unique properties that can potentially address some of the problems of accessibility and trustworthiness. These include distributed governance, which ensures that no single entity controls the network; open access, which allows anybody with an internet connection to participate; and security through cryptography, which protects the integrity of funds.

Just imagine if you could get all of that — just by using one of these "blockchains"!

---

[*] If you follow the cryptocurrency world, you'll recognise this as a SAFT offering (Simple Agreement for Future Tokens) — a form of Initial Coin Offering that would supposedly not be an offering of securities in US law. The SEC felt otherwise, and won in court against Telegram's SAFT on this point in 2020.

That list of qualities — distributed governance, open access, security through cryptography — was originally a list of claims about Bitcoin. They don't entirely work for Bitcoin either, as we saw in the previous chapter — Bitcoin was centralised by about 2014, access is overwhelmingly via cryptocurrency exchanges acting as shaky financial institutions, and the blockchain itself may be secure, but fraud is rampant.

You'll see blockchain promoters do this a lot — they'll make a list of partially-true claims about Bitcoin, then say that their thing has something to do with blockchain, so their thing must therefore do all of them.

Watch out for blockchain promoters — in this case, Libra's promoters — trying to drive a truckload of assumptions through "can" and "potentially." As in the above quote, they'll slip from a "could" statement to a present-tense "is" statement, as if the made-up thing they just imagined exists right now. Facebook admits later in the white paper that their blockchain won't do all of those things.

Even to the extent that blockchains do these things, existing "decentralised" cryptocurrencies completely fail to scale up to more than toy proof-of-concept transaction rates. Bitcoin and its copies do decentralisation with proof-of-work mining — which can't give usable transaction rates without breaking the security model.

The obvious move is not to decentralise — for example, Ripple Labs' XRP is fast, it uses a network of trusted validators to process transactions, and ultimate control rests with Ripple. Enterprise blockchain systems run entirely on this "permissioned" model. The more ideological crypto fans hate the idea of any central control — but they also have networks that can't scale.

So Facebook proposes a permissioned blockchain, with a list of Libra-endorsed official processing nodes. There are some technical details to mitigate the effects of a compromised validator node, but the Libra Association could eject them from the network by legal means as needed.

This is nothing new — crypto people looked at Facebook's plan, and saw something that was more or less Ripple's XRP with smart contracts. It would be a completely centrally-controlled system, run by a single entity. In fact, nothing that was proposed for Libra actually needed a blockchain.

The initial Libra software release was a bare sketch of the planned system. Elaine Ou at Bloomberg News, who was a long-time Bitcoin fan, tried out the code drop.[60] The software let her put fake coins into a simple cryptocurrency wallet. She was surprised how unfinished the code was, given that it came with "a 12-page white paper accompanied by 96 pages of technical detail," and how badly this compared to previous software releases by Facebook.

(Ou's guess was that Libra must have been released early to appease financial regulators — because the code drop was useless to technologists. As it turned out, the Libra documentation for regulators was just as primitive — which left people wondering just what Facebook's blockchain unit had been doing all this time.)

Libra's creators really wanted Libra to be Bitcoin, so they wanted to take their energy-efficient blockchain fully permissionless:

> Together with the community, the association will research the technological challenges on the path to a permissionless ecosystem so that we can meet the objective to begin the transition within five years of the launch.

There's obvious issues here. If the Libra blockchain is out of anyone's control, then what's the Libra Association for? How would it keep the Libra currency stable? How would the backing reserve work?

The secondary white paper "Moving Toward Permissionless Consensus" lists these problems — but doesn't have solutions.[61]

But the biggest problem is that all of this is an unsolved problem in computer science — how to do the Bitcoin decentralised governance trick, but without proof-of-work. This is called the "Blockchain Trilemma": how to be all three of decentralised, scalable and secure. Proof-of-work currencies sacrifice scalability.

So far, there are lots of blockchain projects that claim they've pulled off this trick — but no accepted solutions. The stated plans for Libra include, not just technology that doesn't exist yet — but mathematics that doesn't exist yet.

## Libraisation

Libra seemed to be particularly aimed at countries that had lots of Facebook users, and also had unstable currencies. David Marcus routinely mentioned how bad Argentina's local currency was when he talked about Libra — he seemed to be thinking of Argentina as a good target for having its currency replaced by Libra.

The Libra plan has obvious money-laundering hazards. "Know Your Customer" (KYC) rules require anyone transmitting currency — or currency substitutes — to track the sources of funds, so as to cut off funding for criminals and terrorists. (The Libra plans for a "digital identity" would almost certainly tie into this.)

Facebook said that Libra would keep to the highest of KYC standards — but one Libra partner being sloppy would risk compromising the whole Libra system, given that the basic aim was to move money around the world at the speed of cryptocurrencies. If the Libra Association couldn't keep this tight, and show developed-world regulators that it had done so, holes like this would be exploited immediately, and place the entire Libra system at risk.

But that brings with it another hazard: the potential Libraisation of local economies. Unplanned dollarisation — when US dollars take over from local currencies — can cause crippling depreciation of the local currency. Libra risked doing the same — but faster. Dollarisation is slowed by the need for physical dollars — which is why the $100 note is so popular internationally — but a vast supply of Libra tokens could be poured into an economy from outside, just by phone.

This would most affect the local poor who couldn't pass KYC checks for access to the Libra system — that is, literally the unbanked that Facebook said it wanted Libra to serve. Libraisation would set up a Libra economy that worked only for the local middle to upper classes — and for rich visitors from other countries.

Blockchains don't solve settlement and compliance issues — they're only more efficient if they can bypass regulation. Libra could only be more efficient than existing systems as long as it could dodge regulation, and none of its competitors could.

Libra could either give 1.7 billion people access, or it could maintain KYC integrity at all Libra access points — it couldn't do both.

## The shadow bank of Libra

Shadow banking is the creation of money as credit, but outside the usual regulations that apply to banks. Shadow banks tend to play fast and loose — because the lack of regulation is their competitive advantage. This leads to problems if shadow banking gets big enough to be a systemic risk — money-market funds and similar non-banks allowing too much easy credit fueled the housing bubble in the lead-up to the 2008 financial crisis, and the shadow banks going bad caused the 2008 credit crunch. In fact, the term "shadow banking" was coined in 2007 to describe this crisis as it was happening.[62]

The Libra token would be a synthetic foreign exchange derivative — a thing that the Libra Association issued, with a value that the Libra Association calculated from the basket of national currencies. It wouldn't have an intrinsic value from the fact of a reserve, as Facebook repeatedly claimed — it would only have a value insofar as the Libra Association said it did. To do this in the US, you need to be a bank, or have your token or share registered as an investment scheme.

So the Libra plan would mean operating as a shadow bank — issuing Libra-denominated liabilities that are explicitly intended to function as money. Libra "will create a mirror banking system using your money," said Carlos Maslatón, the head of treasury at Libra member Xapo, when he was explaining the plan in a private WhatsApp chat group.[63]

Facebook's bitcoiners wanted to create unregulated credit as a shadow bank themselves — because they were sure that they were smarter than all those conventional mainstream economists, and wouldn't set off a disaster. Libra's creators spent much of 2019 and early 2020 insisting that Libra couldn't possibly cause problems from shadow banking — even though it was obvious to everyone else that shadow banking followed directly from the Libra plan.

## Libra's ideal world: liberty for me

The white paper also set out Libra's ideological goals. This is what Facebook said it wanted from Libra:

> We believe that many more people should have access to financial services and to cheap capital.

> We believe that people have an inherent right to control the fruit of their legal labor.

> We believe that global, open, instant, and low-cost movement of money will create immense economic opportunity and more commerce across the world.

> We believe that people will increasingly trust decentralized forms of governance.

> We believe that a global currency and financial infrastructure should be designed and governed as a public good.

We believe that we all have a responsibility to help advance financial inclusion, support ethical actors, and continuously uphold the integrity of the ecosystem.

These seem largely unexceptionable in terms of conventional market liberalism — though the odd turns of phrase in the second and fourth items in that list should bring to the reader's attention Libra's ancestry in Bitcoin, in Murray Rothbard's completely unregulated anarcho-capitalism, and in the world of Silicon Valley venture capital.

The Libra plan came out when Facebook was under increasingly close attention from governments, who were deeply suspicious of the company's track record on privacy, election manipulation and falsified news. Facebook had repeatedly defied calls to answer to elected representatives — such as the company's open defiance of parliamentary subpoenas from the United Kingdom and from Canada.

And yet, Facebook seemed to think it was large enough, and powerful enough, to swing a coup against the concept of government control of money.

Libra is an attempt to fulfill the ideological aims of Bitcoin, as seen by venture capitalists and rich anarcho-capitalists who resent the very concept of regulation or oversight — by issuing their own fast-moving private money in quantities large enough that they can't be stopped.

In the secondary Libra white paper "Commitment to Compliance and Consumer Protection," Facebook directly stated that its intent was "to shape a regulatory environment"[64] — Facebook wanted to *shape* regulation, not work to existing regulation. Regulators would need to bend to Facebook.

The white paper says: "The Libra Blockchain is pseudonymous and allows users to hold one or more addresses that are not linked to their real-world identity." This is normal in cryptocurrency — Bitcoin fans consider it a feature — but it's directly at odds with Know Your Customer requirements. Perhaps they meant this for users with large amounts of funds that they'd like to stash away, out of sight, on the Libra blockchain.

From the viewpoint of Libra's Bitcoin origins, "an inherent right to control the fruit of their legal labor" comes across as Libra members' aspirations to swing the power of their capital as they please. Venture capital firms with their own Libra validators, able to exchange Libra tokens between themselves directly — out of sight of regulation or taxation.

These ideas have circulated in Silicon Valley for a while. Facebook board member and advisor Peter Thiel started PayPal with the idea of freeing money from government oversight — just like Bitcoin a decade later. In a 1999 speech to PayPal staff, Thiel said:[65]

> Of course, what we're calling "convenient" for American users will be revolutionary for the developing world … PayPal will give citizens worldwide more direct control over their currencies than they ever had before. It will be nearly impossible for corrupt governments to steal wealth from their people through their old means — because if they try, the people will switch to dollars or pounds or yen, in effect dumping the worthless local currency for something more secure.
>
> … I have no doubt that this company has the chance to become the Microsoft of payments, the financial operating system of the world.

Facebook had all these ambitions for Libra.

This all points to the real attraction of the project for Facebook. Libra isn't really for consumers — Libra is Facebook's call to arms against the very notion of regulation. Facebook wants to be too big to regulate, and lead the way for its Silicon Valley fellows to be too big to regulate.

Governments and regulators immediately understood what Libra was trying to do — and that's why, within hours of the announcement, they called for a ban on the entire scheme. It's one thing when some silly ICO says this stuff — but it's quite another coming from a company that already thinks it's beyond any oversight.

# Chapter 6:
# Banking the unbanked

Without the help of all, he can do nothing, although his
strong-boxes are full of gold.

— Peter Kropotkin[66]

Banking the unbanked — reducing financial exclusion — has been
acknowledged as a public welfare issue for decades, in both rich and
poor countries. If you're not in the system, you're not part of society.

Facebook and WhatsApp have billions of users in the developing
world — but these users don't generate much income for Facebook.
A lot of them don't even have bank accounts. Maybe Libra could get
these users into an economy that Facebook could tap into.

The problems Facebook claims to solve with Libra are real.
International remittance fees are around 6.7% of the money being
sent. Mobile money is the cheapest channel, with fees of around
3.3% — with the poorest and least-connected paying the most.[67]

Facebook was clear in Libra's mission statement:

Libra's mission is to enable a simple global currency and
financial infrastructure that empowers billions of people.

Facebook's very first promise was that Libra would give the
unbanked meaningful participation in the financial system — and so
it was vital that everyone should support Libra to this end. But they
didn't specify at all how Libra would do this.

## The missing white paper

Most other concepts in the main Libra white paper had secondary
white papers that went into more detail — but Facebook's plans to
bank the unbanked didn't. The Libra plan has never been set out in
writing.

It was near-impossible to get meaningful detail from Facebook on
just how Libra would bank the unbanked — almost as if they weren't
quite sure either.

Around the June 2019 announcement of Libra, Kevin Weil —
Calibra/Novi's vice president of product, and one of the three listed
authors of the Libra white paper — spoke of WhatsApp users in

developing countries sending each other photos of money transfer receipts. His press slogan at the time was: "We want to make sending money as easy as sending a text message."[68]

Weil would later talk at conferences about the idea of Libra as a universal standard payment system — like the Internet, but for money — and that this would help bank the unbanked. He put these plans "decades" out, which made his ideas conveniently untestable, and not just vague.[69]

## Blockchains and banking the unbanked

At the pre-announcement press conference for Libra on Monday 17 June, David Marcus said that Libra would solve the problem of billions of people not having bank accounts. He told the press how the problems of banking the unbanked were technical — that banks were unable to move money fast enough without a blockchain.

This is completely backwards. Banks know how to move numbers between computers. The slow part is settlement and compliance — making sure that everything is done in order, and making sure that banks, and money transmitters in general, are solvent, honest and not fronting for drug runners.

The phrase "bank the unbanked" was picked up by the Bitcoin subculture in about 2013, as something that Bitcoin would obviously do. Later cryptocurrencies made the same claim.

Nobody in Bitcoin, or any later cryptocurrency, has ever presented a coherent path from the existence of their crypto to financial inclusion.

Facebook seems to have lifted the claim directly from the Bitcoin subculture — and they supplied just as little detail.

The Libra plan as presented was — in its entirety — that a blockchain-based currency accessible on a phone would solve the problem. This would enable a system to evolve that would do the hard bits — because a blockchain could apparently do this with lower fees, just by existing. It's literally the Bitcoin claim, just with a different name for the coin.

## Banking the unbanked in rich countries

The Libra white paper conflated the unbanked in developing countries with the unbanked in developed countries — specifically, the US. This is a completely different local problem.

The poor have enormous trouble getting bank accounts in the US. Banks will often refuse customers who they think might cause the slightest regulatory trouble. And if you've ever had a bank account shut, you might not be able to get a new account.

The practical solutions that work to get the US unbanked into the system are sociological, and involve one-to-one on-the-ground work — walking people through basic financial literacy, and how to find an account that works for them.[70] In many countries, banks are required to offer no-fee basic accounts.

And there's nothing wrong with the US dollar for banking the US unbanked — creating a new currency is not in any way a necessary step. If Facebook really cared about banking the unbanked, it could have set up a foundation to do this any time in the past ten years.

Banking the unbanked is a social process. Marcus and the white paper speak as if any of this is a technology problem — and none of it is.

## Banking the unbanked in poor countries

The poor are poor, not stupid — and their living conditions are different in each country. You can't impose a system top-down from your office in Menlo Park — you need to work locally.

The Libra white paper figure of 1.7 billion unbanked comes from the World Bank report *The Global Findex Database, 2017: Measuring Financial Inclusion and the Fintech Revolution.*[71] Chapter 6 is "Opportunities For Expanding Financial Inclusion Through Digital Technology" — this is where Facebook read up on the problem.

But page 89 points out that a mobile phone isn't enough — you need financial infrastructure on the ground, and a reliable system to cash out through. Page 93 notes that three-quarters of those 1.7 billion people don't have Internet access, even if they have a mobile phone — and whether it's a smartphone that can run apps, such as the Calibra/Novi wallet, isn't specified in the *Global Findex Database*.

Consider M-Pesa — a service from mobile phone provider Vodafone, one of the initial Libra Association members. M-Pesa started from the ground up in Kenya in 2005, for a customer base with 2G mobile phones with no data and no apps, and a 72% adult literacy rate. M-Pesa's slogan was "Send money home" — domestic remittances. Users of Vodafone's local operator Safaricom could put money on account at a Safaricom shop, send a text message, and the receiver could show the message to get the cash from another Safaricom shop.

This sounds simple — but an easy system for users always has a complicated system at the back end. As well as technology, the project had to deal with finance, culture, politics and regulation — running a network of agents, giving agents incentives that worked and didn't distort the system, balancing and redistributing cash on hand, and limiting fraud.

M-Pesa worked because it started from what its users needed — rather than starting from a solution, like "bank accounts" or "blockchains," and trying to find a question that solution could answer.[72]

By 2019, M-Pesa had 37 million customers. But it never really took off in India[73] or South Africa[74] because banks already had good market penetration — and it failed in Romania and Albania because the informal, off the books, cash in hand economy was around 30% of GDP,[75] and people relying on shadow economies aren't so keen on electronic trackability.[76] Local conditions are local.

Another issue for the unbanked is paperwork. The *Global Findex Database* reports 20% to 49% of adults without a bank account don't have the documentation needed to open one. Others report just … not having enough money to use a bank account. A Silicon Valley app and a blockchain aren't going to solve either of these.

# Cash, privacy and banking the unbanked

Physical cash has the advantage of privacy — the bank and the tax office can't trace the movement of every note and coin. Only large transactions require notification to the anti-money-laundering (AML) authorities.

People with money, who benefit from being part of the system, don't worry nearly as much about traceability — they care much more about convenience than whether their bank has a copy of their entire financial life. The promoters of schemes to bank the unbanked tend to be from this social class.

Privacy of cash is a feature for the poor and marginalised in the informal economy, not just for the crooks that AML rules are supposedly intended to block — because being poor is treated by the middle-class as inherently suspect, and things the poor do may be criminalised *because* it's the poor doing them.

The poor would mostly love to be part of the system — they want more secure and stable material circumstances, and to feel like respectable members of society. But often, they can't get into the system even when they want to. So the poor and marginalised need the informal and marginal economy — that isn't fully legible to the authorities — to survive.

Making people visible to the system, but not giving them power and security within the system, is a direct threat to them. The greatest day-to-day enemy of the poor is the middle-class bureaucrat who contemptuously treats them as data to be processed, without care to their needs or circumstances. James C. Scott's book *Seeing Like A State* describes the process:[77]

> The working poor were often the first subjects of scientific social planning. Schemes for improving their daily lives were promulgated by progressive urban and public-health policies and instituted in model factory towns and newly founded welfare agencies. Subpopulations found wanting in ways that were potentially threatening — such as indigents, vagabonds, the mentally ill, and criminals — might be made the objects of the most intensive social engineering.

Several past electronic money systems failed because having your informal economy fully legible to the state is not a feature — M-Pesa's failed push into Romania and Albania is a good example. So much is done by barter — both to stay off the books, and because they just don't have the cash. It's a substantially non-cash economy. M-Pesa failed to read the room.

Large parts of the Greek economy operate similarly, which is why the Greek government is so desperate to get more people off cash and onto electronic payment systems — to get transactions into legible, taxable form.

Can Libra solve any of this? There are no signs that Facebook even understands this is an issue.

## Libra scales the ivory tower

Libra was created by well-off-to-rich bitcoiners from the venture capital and startup world, creating a system for people whose lives they only understood in terms of their own — and the system they came up with coincidentally looked very like a way for rich venture capitalists with anarcho-capitalist leanings to shift large sums around out of sight.

"Bank the unbanked" looked like an excuse slapped on top of that — even as the proposers seem to have been completely sincere in this aspiration.

"Banking the unbanked" is a complicated process that needs to adapt to local conditions. Facebook didn't say anything about their plan to do this — so regulators looked at the rest of the Libra plan, that didn't make sense in poor countries, and seemed to be a plan to set up an ill-regulated shadow bank in rich countries.

# Chapter 7:
# The Libra Reserve plan
# and economic stability

You can't really build a global stablecoin, right? It's an oxymoron.

— Christian Catalini[82]

The original Libra plan was to issue Libra currency tokens, each fully backed by assets held in reserve by the Libra Association. The value of a Libra token would be calculated from a basket of national currencies in the reserve.

The revised and cut-down 2020 "Libra 2.0" plan was to just use national currency tokens — a dollar token, a euro token and so on — running on the Libra blockchain. This would still have a version of its Libra basket token, based on these national tokens.

But either way, there's a serious problem — Facebook has 2.5 billion users across all of its services. What would it mean if a substantial fraction of Facebook users started using Libra? Just how much money would there be in the reserve?

The Libra reserve might be on the order of a trillion dollars — one of the largest single investment funds in the world, larger than any single country's entire sovereign wealth fund. Could the Libra reserve be a *systemic* risk, that could damage whole national economies?

This problem was immediately obvious to every regulator, banker and financial journalist. Facebook just insisted it surely wouldn't be a problem.

Issuing tokens to represent a currency, based on a backing reserve, was obviously banking — and if it wasn't, then it was issuing investment securities. Facebook denied they wanted Libra to be a bank, even as their plan was, literally, to do things only banks were allowed to do.

## The man behind the plan

Christian Catalini is a professor of business at MIT, Head Economist at Novi and Chief Economist at the Libra Association.

He is credited as a co-creator of Libra. The economic plan for Libra was put together by Catalini.

Catalini's academic work focuses on blockchains, cryptocurrencies and crowdfunding. He has written numerous theoretical papers on how blockchain economics could work. In 2014, he supervised an experiment to promote Bitcoin by giving incoming MIT students $100 worth of bitcoins each — and was disconcerted to find that even the few who bothered claiming the bitcoins tended to just sell them.[78]

When Facebook started looking into blockchains, Catalini spoke to Morgan Beller and David Marcus about their plans. He liked their ideas — "if a company with the engineering talent and reach and scale of Facebook were to design this right and really build a platform around financial inclusion and payments, it could have a transformative impact on the globe"[79] — and took leave from his MIT position to start at Facebook in July 2018.

The Libra reserve white paper[59] does not list any references. However, some commenters noted how much the plan for Libra resembled Austrian School economist Friedrich von Hayek's 1976 book *The Denationalisation of Money*,[80] in which he advocates competing private corporate currencies, and assumes the public will prefer whichever has the lowest inflation.

# How the Libra reserve works

In the original plan, each token of the Libra currency would be backed by a basket of currencies — assets denominated in a selection of national currencies, in fixed proportions. The second plan, for tokens to represent the national currencies, was much the same.

Facebook never stated the proportions they were thinking of for the basket. One report in September 2019 said Facebook had told Fabio De Masi (Left Party, Germany) that it would be 50% US dollar, 18% euro, 14% Japanese yen, 11% pound sterling and 8% Singapore dollar.[58][81] Catalini later said the percentages were "just a proposal."[82]

The assets in the reserve would be bank accounts, government bonds, and similar low-risk, liquid assets. Not quite cash-equivalents — but close enough that they could be cashed in as quickly as was needed to redeem the Libra tokens.

End users would not get interest on the money tied up in tokens — instead, the interest would pay for running the Libra system. Anything left over would be distributed as dividends to Association members who held Libra Investment Tokens.

The reserve wouldn't really be a backing for the currency tokens — the only link between a token on your phone and the Libra reserve would be that the Libra Association said there was a link. You would *not* have a direct claim on the reserve itself. You could only get the token's claimed value in real money from an authorised Libra vendor. One token would only be exchangeable for actual money if an authorised vendor would give you actual money for it.

Most people would just buy and sell one currency — the Reserve white paper doesn't say how the Association planned to deal with imbalances if one of the basket currencies was much more popular than the others. Nor the swarms of foreign exchange trading bots that would be unleashed the moment Libra was released, if wallets like Facebook's Calibra/Novi really didn't charge any fee. There was nothing on how the Association would deal with the foreign exchange risk it would be taking on, trying to keep the basket balanced.

## What is a Libra?

Regulators don't look so much at what a company calls a financial instrument. They look at what the company wants to do with the instrument, and what existing thing the instrument seems to be.

There have been a few previous basket-based currencies, or at least basket-based units of account — which isn't quite the same thing. The best-known is probably the International Monetary Fund (IMF)'s Special Drawing Right (SDR), made of a basket of currencies heavily used in trade. Since October 2016, the SDR has been 41.73% US dollar, 30.93% euro, 10.92% Chinese yuan, 8.33% Japanese yen and 8.09% pound sterling. So Libra's basket is a lot like the SDR basket without the yuan.

The SDR is a way of keeping the accounts for a reserve — it's not a currency, as such. The IMF and the Bank for International Settlements (BIS) give all their accounts in SDRs.

Since the SDR was created, nobody has started a currency based on SDRs, businesses don't trade in SDRs, banks don't offer accounts denominated in SDRs — in daily life, everyone just works in national currencies. The euro started as a similar sort of basket, but almost nobody used it for anything until it evolved into a currency in its own right. It's not clear there would be demand for Libra's basket offering.

Libra's plan to issue a new currency unit backed by a basket of currencies closely resembles an existing financial instrument — an exchange-traded fund (ETF). An organisation has a pool of investment, and sells shares in the pool; the only link between the pool of investment and the shares in the pool is that the organisation says there's a link.

Shares in ETFs are closely regulated as investments — the shares can't just flow around like a currency.

An ETF will have its investment assets held in trust by a custodian — the ETF's managing company can't just dip into the assets if they get in trouble. This would be *more* protection than Libra promises.

If the Libra association only issues tokens representing national currencies, then that turns Libra from something very like an ETF into something very like a money market fund (MMF).

Money market funds could be called the original version of the "stablecoin"[83] — MMFs take deposits, invest them in safe securities such as US Treasury bills or short-term commercial paper, and pay the investors dividends. Money market funds in the US were regulated by the SEC as offerings of securities, but they accepted deposits in a very bank-like manner, and were regarded as nearly as secure and cash-equivalent as banks — even though your money was at risk.

The money market funds weren't regulated as closely as banks. So they loaded up on other investments that were rated as very low risk. This led to huge new demand for cash-equivalent investments — which led to companies like Lehman Bros creating new "cash equivalent" AAA-rated "secure" investments to meet the demand.

Many of these turned out to be backed only by questionable mortgages. Then the investments went bad in the 2008 financial crisis, and several large money market funds had to be bailed out.

Since then, regulators have been exceedingly cautious of MMF-like proposals — the US and Europe have spent the last decade tightening the rules on money market funds.

Libra would have tremendous difficulty avoiding being regulated as either a security (ETF or MMF) or a bank.

## The white elephant in the room

Facebook knows that regulators will demand the reserves keep 1:1 backing, and monitor the backing to make sure it stays 1:1. But a large reserve is a powerful lever in itself. Regulators' big worry about the Libra reserve is that Facebook users number in the billions — so the reserve might be weighty enough to affect entire financial systems.

How large would the Libra reserve be? TenPay/WeChat Pay and Alipay in China held a total of 1 trillion yuan ($151 billion) of customer funds as of June 2018,[84] for approximately one billion users

— that being just the working float of customer money in the system. On the other hand, total e-money float across all providers in the Euro area in 2019 hovered around only 14 billion euros [85] — because users kept their money in banks.

With up to two billion Libra users, the working float for the Libra reserve might be small like Europe, or it might be large as in China — regulators had to be ready for a Libra reserve on the scale of a trillion dollars. If people kept their savings in Libra, the reserve could be much larger. One European Central Bank paper estimated the Libra reserve as likely to be between €153 billion and €3 trillion [86] — "Libra could potentially become one of Europe's largest MMFs."

How big are national wealth reserves? The world's largest sovereign wealth fund is Norway's Government Pension Fund Global, more commonly known as the Oil Fund, at approximately US$1.1 trillion. The main fund stabilising the Singapore dollar is GIC Private Limited, estimated at US$453 billion.[87] (The other Singaporean fund is Temasek, slightly smaller at US$210 billion, which later joined the Libra Association.)

Libra would operate at this sort of scale. A trillion dollar investment fund is more than enough to affect the financial system. Regulators realised this immediately, even as Facebook remained in denial.

(As Libra's reserve might dwarf the Singapore dollar's entire reserve, let alone its cash-equivalent securities, the currency was a bizarre choice for the Libra basket. This is probably why the Singapore dollar was left out of the 2020 Libra 2.0 plan.)

Facebook didn't seem to understand that the Libra reserve's sheer weight could be a problem. Their public statements assumed that the reserve would have no effect on the currencies in the basket — or on the governments they planned to buy stable cash-equivalent investments from. Both claims were obviously wrong if Libra operated at Facebook scale.

# Throwing your weight around, one-to-one

There are several obvious side-effects of a trillions-of-dollars float just wandering around the markets, looking for something to do with itself.

## Soaking up all the cash-equivalents

A currency might have a large circulating supply, but there's a lot less cash-equivalent investments in a given currency for you to just casually go out and buy. We noted above how, in the run-up to the 2008 financial crisis, new "cash-equivalent" investments were created that weren't nearly as safe as the government cash-equivalents they were substitutes for — because the actually-safe investments had already been bought up. And this was in the US dollar, a large currency for a large economy.

Libra could easily soak up all the cash-equivalent paper. Just the task of keeping Libra stable would be quite enough to move currency and bond markets.[88] The Libra Association would be able to pressure governments to issue sufficient government paper to back Libra's reserve — whether it was in the interest of the government's citizens, or not.

And if those "cash-equivalents" went bad — as they did in the 2008 crisis — there would be a run on the no-longer-fully-backed Libra reserve.

The least disruptive solution would be for governments to require the Libra reserve to be deposited directly with the central bank at zero interest — much as the People's Bank of China requires the large money transmitters to keep 100% of customer deposits in a zero-interest account directly with the central bank.[89] The Bank of England has suggested something similar for Libra-like stablecoins.

## Taking up all the deposits

If Libra pulls large quantities of deposits out of commercial banks and into the Libra reserve, then that money won't be available as reserves for the banks — and this would affect banks' ability to make loans, which keep the real economy running smoothly,[90] and to invest their reserve, which might mean they would have to raise interest rates on loans.

This runs the risk of a credit squeeze — which was how the 2008 financial crisis really did its damage.

A credit squeeze from a lack of commercial bank deposits is also one of the worries that central banks have about central bank digital currencies. But central banks have a mandate to maintain economic stability — private companies don't.

## An end-run around capital controls

Capital controls limit the flow of money in and out of small economies, in the interest of local stability.

Capital controls were strongly discouraged for many years by the United States, the IMF, and the World Bank, in the interest of global free trade — and by the owners of substantial amounts of capital, who wanted to move their money as freely as possible, and never mind the effects on everyone else.

So central banks had to solve an "impossible trinity" — a reasonably stable exchange rate, an independent local monetary policy, *and* free capital flows. If a country tries to pursue all three at once, things may go well at first, but will soon become unstable.

A good example is the Asian crisis of 1997–1998 — where countries tried to keep their local currencies pegged to the US dollar, allow free capital flow, and set their interest rates independently. At this time, local interest rates were higher than in the US — so, with no capital controls, foreign money was promptly moved wherever it could grow fastest. Investors took huge profits.

When trade balances shifted, and local interest rates dropped, the foreign investors took their money out just as quickly as they'd put it in. Countries such as Thailand ran out of dollars, and had to let their currencies float, and thus devalue. But many short-term debts were in US dollars — and this bankrupted local businesses.

The crisis spread to other countries, and the IMF had to bail them out. Since the Asian crisis, the IMF and World Bank have been more receptive to the use case for capital controls.

Facebook explicitly listed breaking capital controls as a goal for Libra in the white paper:

> We believe that global, open, instant, and low-cost movement of money will create immense economic opportunity and more commerce across the world.

As an internationally frictionless private currency founded by millionaires and billionaires, Libra would mostly be used, not by individuals to buy goods and services — but by people like its founders to move capital with much greater ease.

Evading capital controls is strongly promoted by the Bitcoin subculture as a use case for cryptocurrency — as Libra's creators well know. The original Libra plan would have made large flows of capital effectively unrestricted, in a much more liquid form than Bitcoin.

## Banking from the shadows

Investing the float of customer funds — that they shouldn't be touching — is a major income stream for many "fintech" startups.

They take in as much customer money as possible, then they manage it like a bank — but without the oversight that banks work under.[91]

The People's Bank of China clamped down on even the possibility of this happening with the requirement for the large money transmitters to deposit 100% of customer funds with the central bank — they didn't want to risk WeChat Pay or Alipay slipping into shadow banking.

Facebook sought only US money transmitter licenses for Calibra — not a banking license — because Calibra/Novi would work like PayPal: a site that holds your money for you to use at your convenience.

But Facebook wants the Libra Association to do bank-like things in the background — take other people's money, and issue credit slips that they say can be used as money. That's a banking activity.

Banks can do all sorts of things with other people's money. They can invest it, loan it out, and offer financial products, for their own benefit. But society has very particular ideas about how you should handle what is, in fact, other people's money — so banks are closely regulated to make sure they're honest, to check they aren't risking their customers' money, and to check they aren't throwing their economic weight around to the point where there are risks to the system.

Non-banks who handle other people's money would love to do the stuff that banks do. Shadow banking is attractive because it isn't as regulated as banking, and doesn't worry about deposit insurance and so on — so shadow banks can offer better interest rates, and financial products that banks aren't allowed to.

Shadow banking is dangerous. Regulators really don't like anything that smells of shadow banking, because they remember the 2008 financial crisis. The house price bubble of the 2000s was fueled by what was effectively credit from non-banks, such as the money market funds — as long as prices kept going up, even bad mortgages could be paid off by the rise in the value of the house if the mortgagee defaulted. Total assets managed by non-banks grew almost as large as the total managed by regulated banks.

When house prices stopped going up and bad mortgages started defaulting, companies wanted their money back. They tried to get their investments out of the non-banks, and these bank runs on non-banks left the non-banks bankrupt and the investors high and dry. This caused a chain of crises in other parts of finance that were relying on the non-banks.[92] The Federal Reserve eventually had to bail out the shadow banking system.

Ant Financial, the parent company of Alipay in China, sells a wide variety of financial products to its users — banking, credit cards, loans, wealth management, insurance. Libra resellers, such as Calibra/Novi, could become some of the world's largest financial services companies.

What services will Libra resellers offer? Will the Libra Association offer the resellers assistance with liquidity — lending them Libra tokens to keep the tokens flowing — the way that central banks do for commercial banks? In the regulated system, this is what allows banks to create money — but under regulation and monitoring.

It's hard to imagine Facebook putting bank-like levels of monitoring into place from the start. By offering financial services without the regulation for those services, Libra turns into a shadow banking system.

It's not at all clear that Facebook understands the obvious implications of what they're saying — but the implications still follow.

Swiss regulators have confirmed that an organisation controlling a Libra-like reserve for a stablecoin pegged to a variable basket of currencies, with interest on the reserve going to the organisation, would need to be run as a bank[93] — Libra's basket plan would absolutely have required a bank charter in Switzerland, and likely in every other jurisdiction it wanted Libra tokens to be allowed into. Even a stablecoin based on national currencies would require regulation as a bank, and the reserves for the coin would be treated as bank deposits.

Before Libra, Bitcoin also promised to solve the problems of the existing financial system and get rid of its middlemen — and then it recreated most of those middlemen, but incompetently.

## Interest? What interest?

The countries whose currencies would be in the Libra basket are running at historically low interest rates. Cash-equivalents, government bonds, and even many corporate bonds in US dollars or euros presently have near-zero, or even negative, interest rates.

JP Morgan Chase fixed-income strategist Joshua Younger wrote to clients on 5 September 2019 about Libra, saying that it was "unclear how such a system could continue to function if the collateral is a cost rather than a revenue source."[94]

Younger also worried that a popular Libra-like coin could make bad economic times worse, not better: "The need to impose transaction costs as rates decline — especially when they turn negative — could worsen and prolong recessions by acting as an escalating tax on consumers and businesses as conditions worsen."

The lack of profit on high-quality cash-equivalent investments would be a strong incentive for the Libra Association to get into riskier but more profitable investments — and make it harder for users to cash out Libra tokens, so as to keep the reserve as large as possible.

If the Libra Association makes up this shortfall by charging fees on Libra wallets, users are likely to leave Libra as fast as they can. When the Bundesbank, the German central bank, was charging negative interest to its local retail banks in late 2019, even those banks started filling bank vaults with physical euro notes.[95]

The Libra 2.0 plan took heed of this objection. The Libra Association members — *i.e.*, Facebook — would subsidise the reserve and transaction costs if needed, and keep tokens convertible back and forth with the base currencies themselves. That is, Facebook wanted so very much to run its own private currency that it would do so at a loss.

## Regulators: Libra shall not pass

In September 2019, the French and German finance ministers both said they could not allow the development of Libra on European soil — as it would really obviously affect their monetary sovereignty.

Bruno Le Maire and Olaf Scholz, the French and German finance ministers, said in a joint statement after a meeting in Helsinki of eurozone finance ministers on September 13: "France and Germany consider that the Libra project, as set out in Facebook's blueprint, fails to convince that those risks will be properly addressed."[96] Scholz said on September 17: "We cannot accept a parallel currency. You have to reject that clearly."[97]

David Marcus responded with a series of tweets that showed no understanding of the issues with the reserve:[98]

> Recently there's been a lot of talk about how Libra could threaten the sovereignty of Nations when it comes to money. I wanted to take the opportunity to debunk that notion.

Libra is designed to be a better payment network and system running on top of existing currencies, and delivering meaningful value to consumers all around the world.

Libra will be backed 1:1 by a basket of strong currencies. This means that for any unit of Libra to exist, there must be the equivalent value in its reserve.

As such there's no new money creation, which will strictly remain the province of sovereign Nations.

We also believe strong regulatory oversight preventing the Libra Association from deviating from its full 1:1 backing commitment is desirable.

Marcus asserted — as he had all through discussion of the Libra project — that issuing a token with a one-to-one full reserve would be sufficient not to affect the stability of economies, even if done at Facebook's scale.

Christian Catalini maintained that "a relatively small level of reserves could support an extremely high volume of transactions. Reserves will grow slowly and would still probably remain small relative to domestic markets."[99] This was despite comparable — and much-discussed — real-world examples such as WeChat Pay and Alipay.

Libra communications chief Dante Disparte said Le Maire and Scholz just didn't understand the blockchain: "We recognize that blockchain is an emerging technology, and that policymakers must carefully consider how its applications fit into their financial system policies."[100]

But the regulators didn't care about the technology at all — the system could have used a conventional SQL database, or paper ledger books. (And Le Maire was actually a fan of blockchains, and had spoken at Paris Blockchain Week!) The regulators were worried by what Facebook was saying, and what Facebook was planning to do with money and financial systems — whatever the back-end technology.

# Chapter 8:
# Libra, privacy and your digital identity

> Facebook and a cartel of junior partners will leverage their platform power to establish a global financial surveillance system, on the back of public monetary systems.
>
> — Raúl Carrillo, Demand Progress[101]

Facebook really wants to do a private currency. Facebook wants to do a private currency so very much that the amended Libra 2.0 white paper of April 2020 — part of Libra's formal application to the Swiss Financial Markets Authority — says that Libra Association members, *i.e.*, Facebook, will top up the reserve with a capital buffer, and the Libra Association, *i.e.*, Facebook, will redeem tokens on the Libra network for cash itself if Libra's vendor network won't.

What does Facebook want from a private currency so much that they're offering to lose money to run it?

The obvious answer is: personal data — because Facebook *always* wants personal data. Facebook's business is selling personal data to advertisers.

Libra would be a massive data mining apparatus sitting atop the financial system. The data is there — it would be completely out of character for Facebook not to collect all the data from Libra that it possibly could.

Would Facebook break Mark Zuckerberg's promises not to use spending data from its Calibra/Novi wallet for ad targeting? Past behaviour is the best predictor of future behaviour — so we should expect that Facebook will break these promises. Facebook does not take "no" or "never" for an answer. We should assume that one of Zuckerberg's key goals with the Libra project is to harvest as much personal data as possible.

## Facebook's track record with privacy

Facebook's reach is massive. Just in the US, 68% of all US adults used Facebook in 2016, and 52% of all US adults used it at least once a day.[102] That's a huge amount of information, often quite private, on a huge number of people.

The Federal Trade Commission's 2019 complaint against Facebook describes how Facebook manages user permissions:[103]

> To encourage users to share information, Facebook promises users that they can control the privacy of their information through Facebook's privacy settings. However, through at least June 2018, Facebook subverted users' privacy choices to serve its own business interests.

Facebook allowed unrestricted access to user profiles, despite the company claiming that apps "will access only the profile information these applications need to operate". Facebook shared personal information with advertisers — including other users' information that had been set "friends only." Supposedly "deleted" user profiles were not deleted.

Facebook's 2011 settlement with the FTC promised this would not happen again — and Facebook said it would put controls into place to make sure it didn't happen again. Then it happened again.

Facebook uses personal data as a business weapon directly. From at least 2011 to 2015, Facebook would pass data to companies it favoured, and withhold data from companies it didn't — it gave special access to Amazon as they bought so much advertising, but cut off messaging app MessageMe in case it got too popular and competed with Facebook.[104]

When Facebook bought WhatsApp in 2014, it told the European Commission that it would not match Facebook and WhatsApp user data — and, in fact, that it couldn't do so reliably. Then in August 2016, Facebook did it anyway, using users' phone numbers to match them across Facebook and WhatsApp. In May 2017, the Commission fined Facebook €110 million for this — and they were particularly annoyed that Facebook knew in 2014 it could share data between WhatsApp and Facebook in this manner, but had told them otherwise.[105]

Political consultancy Cambridge Analytica compiled data on 50 million Facebook users — who were mostly the friends of 270,000 users who had downloaded a researcher's "personality quiz" app — into comprehensive user profiles that it then used to closely target political advertising in the 2016 US election and the 2016 UK Brexit referendum. It turned out that thousands of other apps had also been scraping third-party personal data since 2008.

The Cambridge Analytica scandal could only happen at all because Facebook allowed access to user data contrary to the users' privacy settings. The UK House of Commons report "Disinformation and 'fake news'" noted that if Facebook had just kept to the 2011 FTC settlement, the Cambridge Analytica scandal could never have happened.[106]

The FTC eventually fined Facebook $5 billion over Cambridge Analytica in 2019 — just before David Marcus appeared before the House and Senate in July.

These are only the most prominent examples. Facebook's history of personal data abuse is extensive, and consistent. Given the chance, you can be sure Facebook will abuse users' data — no matter what permissions the users think they gave, and no matter the promises Facebook may have made to regulators.

## What could Facebook do with data from Novi and Libra?

Facebook dominates social media. Facebook and Google are an advertising duopoly. Facebook has tried to break into payments for years — lured by the prospect of being able to get users' spending habits directly, rather than guessing from their interests and interactions. Using data from Novi to sell targeted advertising would be hugely effective and lucrative.

The question is not what Libra is — but what it can do. And what it's likely to do, given Facebook's history.

Facebook has said that Novi would only share data with the Facebook platform with explicit user consent — but Facebook routinely requires excess data sharing permissions, or includes user "consent" hidden in lengthy terms and conditions.

At no point has Facebook stated that having a Novi wallet will not require you to have a Facebook account. Facebook has previously tied other services to having a Facebook account. The 2020 Oculus Quest 2 virtual reality headset required a Facebook account, and an automated system locked many buyers out, turning their new headset into a "$300 paperweight."[107] All Oculus headsets will require a Facebook account by 2023, to help you "find, connect, and play with friends in VR" — and only incidentally to match you to ads.[108]

Facebook is also likely to just share the Novi data with its other apps anyway — as it did with WhatsApp.

Facebook even builds shadow profiles on Internet users who aren't Facebook users, by using the Facebook buttons included on web pages. All the incentives are for Novi to use a "Pay with Novi" web page button to collect data on non-users, in the same way, and there's nothing to stop them.

The Libra blockchain will be accessible to Libra Association members. Novi will have a copy of the data on the Libra blockchain, and Facebook will be able to use data-matching to fill out shadow profiles of every user of Libra — not just the Novi users.

## Digital papers, please

The most important component of Libra will be digital identity — even more important than monetising your spending data.

We've seen how Know-Your-Customer, as required by anti-money-laundering laws, would cripple Facebook's plans to bank the unbanked.

Libra couldn't work as planned without an internationally accepted digital identity standard. Facebook wants to be the entity backing that digital identity standard.

If you think Facebook is hard to regulate now — just think how hard Facebook would be to regulate if it controlled not just the money, but your access to financial services outside Facebook.

How hard would it be for a government to stop Facebook abusing your personal information any way they liked, or leaking your data to their third-party customers?

## How will Libra work out in practice?

The most likely outcome of Libra is a completely predictable personal data abuse scandal, just like the ones before it — and a public apology from Zuckerberg, using a variant on his standard apology template:

> I hope you understand, this is not how I meant for things to go, and I apologize for any harm done as a result of my neglect to consider how quickly the site would spread and its consequences thereafter. I definitely see how my intentions could be seen in the wrong light.

That was Zuckerberg's apology for using female Harvard students' photos without permission for his site "FaceMash" in 2003. Zuckerberg has used variations of this wording since. Zeynep Tufecki called it Zuckerberg's "14-Year Apology Tour."[109]

David Marcus and Mark Zuckerberg both promised the US House and Senate repeatedly that Novi data would be kept isolated from

Facebook's advertising engine. I see no reason to doubt Marcus's sincerity — but, given Facebook's extensive track record of repeated privacy violations, it would be foolish to assume Zuckerberg didn't have his fingers crossed.

# Chapter 9:
# The regulators recoil in horror

Facebook is doing a great job at spurring regulatory clarity in the industry — alas, in the direction of "ban this and jail everyone involved."

— Ben Munster[110]

In the weeks after the Libra announcement, the financial press, the regulators and the central banks picked over what Facebook had provided and tried to make sense of it — and what its implications were.

Most of the implications were bad. It's one thing to do a small crypto with all sorts of grandiose claims, but which is mostly just going to be traded by crypto speculators — and it's quite another when it's a company the size of Facebook, with billions of users, and a possible trillion-dollar backing reserve.

Mark Zuckerberg said in 2010:[111]

In a lot of ways Facebook is more like a government than a traditional company. We have this large community of people, and more than other technology companies we're really setting policies.

Governments kept Zuckerberg's comparison firmly in mind.

## Why financial regulation exists

If you're handling other people's money, then those other people are going to have very particular ideas on how you handle money. So finance has rules and regulations. You can argue the particular rules — but a functional system that you can do business in is going to have regulations, and regulators to oversee them.

Financial regulators are fine with innovation, and want to encourage and help business development — but they know all the ways that cutting corners can go wrong. Everyone remembers the 2008 financial crisis. Regulators need to know that a big new player knows what it's doing.

If a normal financial institution wants to do something new and unusual, they'll call the regulators *very* early in the process. They'll set out their plans, maybe show them a prototype. If a regulator has concerns, the company will shower them in knowledgeable lawyers to reassure them.

In finance, the process of iterating to a Minimum Viable Product involves regulators at every step of the way.

What you *don't* do is write up a rough sketch of the system with none of the details filled in, announce that billions of people around the world will use it, then throw the rough sketch over the wall — and expect regulators and legislators to be just fine with this. You don't go, "yep, we're doing this, be amazed," like you're announcing a video game or an electric truck.

Facebook spent two years working out their blockchain plan and philosophy — and almost none of this time talking to the financial regulators who could sink their financial product with a word.

Facebook seemed *actually surprised* when all the regulators reacted to their fabulous plans with horror — within hours of them being announced.

## Pre-launch discussions with regulators

Several months before the Libra announcement, Facebook employees met with US Securities and Exchange Commission Chairman Jay Clayton, and with SEC staff, to talk about cryptocurrencies — though not specifically about the project that became Libra.[112]

In spring 2019, David Marcus met with Steve Mnuchin, US Secretary of the Treasury. Even with the few details Facebook had at the time, Mnuchin told Marcus: "I hate everything about this."[17]

In the month or two before the announcement, Facebook began contacting the most important regulators — but gave them only the vaguest details of the project itself.[113]

In the UK, Facebook met with a junior minister at the UK Ministry of Finance, and with officials working on cryptocurrency policy, on 23 April 2019. The next day, Facebook met with the Financial Conduct Authority (FCA) to discuss Libra. On 14 May, Facebook met officials from the Ministry of Finance, the Bank of England and the FCA.[114]

Facebook approached the US Commodities and Futures Trading Commission (CFTC) in late May 2019, to work out whether CFTC rules would apply to Libra.[115]

# Europe

The very first official response to the Libra announcement on 18 June came within minutes — from Bruno Le Maire, France's Minister for Finance. Le Maire was a guest on Europe 1 Radio in France that morning, and said:[116]

> That Facebook creates its own currency, an instrument for transactions, why not. On the other hand, it's out of the question that it becomes a sovereign currency ... The ability to issue financial instruments, to maintain a reserve and to be a lender of last resort — all this is not possible.

> ... I have asked the G7 central bank governors to report to us by mid-July, when the G7 finance ministers meet, so that they can tell us what guarantees to obtain from Facebook. We must ensure that there is no risk for the consumer either.

> This will allow Facebook to collect millions and millions of fragments of data again. This reinforces my conviction that it is necessary to regulate the digital giants, to ensure that they do not end up in monopolistic positions.

After a letter from Le Maire and Banque de France governor François Villeroy de Galhau, the Group of Seven nations (G7) established a working group to consider the risks of private currencies, and "look into a range of challenges raised by the emergence of stable coins, including on the regulatory front."[117] The letter didn't name Libra — but everyone knew Libra was what this was about.

G7 finance ministers met on July 17 and agreed they had "a very large consensus on the need to act quickly."[118] Benoît Cœuré of the European Central Bank presented a first report on Libra, and the G7 asked Cœuré to set up a task force to look into Libra-like currencies.[119]

Cœuré said afterwards: "Market discipline is useful but I wouldn't see it as progress to shift monetary sovereignty from governments to private multinationals ... large companies having enormous market power which occasionally have been indicted of misusing their client data."[120]

# United States

Within hours of Libra's announcement, Maxine Waters, chair of the US House Committee on Financial Services, promised greater regulation of cryptocurrencies in general, starting with Libra:[121]

> With the announcement that it plans to create a cryptocurrency, Facebook is continuing its unchecked expansion and extending its reach into the lives of its users ... Given the company's troubled past, I am requesting that Facebook agree to a moratorium on any movement forward on developing a cryptocurrency until Congress and regulators have the opportunity to examine these issues and take action.

Crypto people routinely call for "regulatory clarity" — meaning, they want permission to do what they were going to do anyway. They're rarely so happy with the clarity they get.

Two days after the Libra announcement, Facebook met with officials from the US Treasury, the SEC and other agencies — and gave them just ... the 12-page Libra white paper. The regulators were shocked that Facebook didn't have detailed answers ready to the obvious questions about money laundering and consumer protection.[122]

Waters and three other House Democrats called on 2 July for Libra to be halted "until regulators and Congress have an opportunity to examine these issues and take action ... If products and services like these are left improperly regulated and without sufficient oversight, they could pose systemic risks that endanger US and global financial stability."[123]

The House Financial Services Committee asked Jerome Powell from the US Federal Reserve about Libra on 10 July. He said that "Libra raises many serious concerns regarding privacy, money laundering, consumer protection and financial stability."[124] The project could not go forward without fully addressing all of these — "in a deliberate process that will not be a sprint to implementation."[125]

Senator Mike Crapo (R-ID) asked Powell if "we need to create a new regulator" to handle Libra-like initiatives. Powell thought this was plausible — since Libra's proposal crossed so many different fields of regulation.[126]

US President Donald Trump tweeted about Libra on 12 July, telling Facebook directly that if they were going to act like a bank, they needed to get a banking charter:[127]

Facebook Libra's "virtual currency" will have little standing or dependability. If Facebook and other companies want to become a bank, they must seek a new Banking Charter and become subject to all Banking Regulations, just like other Banks, both National and International.

Facebook had met with Treasury Department staff on 27 June.[128] Steve Mnuchin gave a press conference on 15 July: "The Treasury Department has expressed very serious concerns that Libra could be misused by money launderers and terrorist financiers … To be clear, FinCEN will hold any entity that transacts in Bitcoin, Libra or any other cryptocurrency to its highest standards." Mnuchin said that "they and others have a lot of work to do before they get us comfortable."[129]

Facebook had registered Calibra with FinCEN, applied for money-transmitter licenses, and applied for a BitLicense — required for cryptocurrency businesses in New York.[130] But that wasn't enough to quiet worries about the Libra system as a whole.

By July, the SEC was already looking into whether Libra would constitute an exchange-traded fund — and hence a security under US law, not a currency or commodity.[128] Jay Clayton said on 16 July that Libra had not approached him since the June announcement. He said, "I am keenly interested in their securities law analysis."[131]

On 14 July, Democratic members of the House Financial Services Committee were circulating a discussion draft of the "Keep Big Tech Out of Finance Act," to maintain "a firewall between commerce and banking." The bill would keep a "large platform utility" — a company primarily offering an online platform service, with at least $25 billion in annual revenue — from offering financial services or launching a "digital asset that is intended to be widely used as [a] medium of exchange."[132] The bill was just a rough draft for discussion, and it wasn't considered likely to make it past the Senate — but it set the tone for the coming House hearing on Libra.

Also in America, Facebook co-founder Chris Hughes warned a few days after the Libra announcement that Libra could move control of monetary policy from banks and governments to private companies — who would put their own business interests ahead of public interests. "What Libra backers are calling 'decentralisation' is in truth a shift of power from developing world central banks toward multinational corporations and the US Federal Reserve and the European Central Bank."[133]

Hughes told regulators to tightly restrict the gateways between Libra and conventional currency. "If global regulators don't act now, it could very soon be too late."

# United Kingdom

Mark Carney, then Governor of the Bank of England, suggested on 20 June that the Bank open deposits to payment providers — as well as the commercial banks it currently dealt with.[134]

Carney mentioned Libra as one such payment provider. Though he cautioned:

> The Bank of England approaches Libra with an open mind but not an open door. Unlike social media for which standards and regulations are being debated well after they have been adopted by billions of users, the terms of engagement for innovations such as Libra must be adopted in advance of any launch ... Our citizens deserve no less.

Carney told a news conference on 11 July: "If you are a systemic payment system, you have to be on all the time. You can't have teething issues, you can't have people losing money out of their wallets ... This is not learning on the job stuff, it's got to be rock solid right from the start or it's not going to start."[135]

The UK's Financial Conduct Authority had got back in touch with Facebook the moment Libra was announced.[136] Andrew Bailey, then head of the FCA, told the Treasury Select Committee on 25 June that the FCA had "already engaged with Facebook and there will be many more engagements. We are waiting to see how the responsibility will divide between Facebook and the other organisation."[137]

# Central banks scramble

A central bank's job is to keep their economy stable against shocks. Central banks reacted to Libra with the same horror that regulators and governments had.

"I think Facebook hadn't thought through carefully how important control of currency is for governments and for central banks," Simon Potter of the Peterson Institute think tank told the Financial Times.

Lael Brainard at the US Federal Reserve concurred: "Libra heightened the urgency and sharpened the focus of senior policymakers on this work."[138]

Stefan Ingves of Riksbank, the Swedish central bank, had looked into a central bank-issued digital krona in 2017. The Libra announcement came as a surprise — central bankers "ended up in a lot of conversations about Libra, because Libra showed up, at least from a central bank perspective, kind of out of the blue."

The Bank for International Settlements (BIS) — the central bank for central banks — warned that "a big tech could be small in financial services and yet rapidly establish a dominant position by leveraging its vast network of users."[139] BIS had a "courtesy meeting" with Facebook before the June announcement — but they knew nothing more than what was in the Libra white papers.[140]

The People's Bank of China (PBOC) said it had been working on a central bank digital currency (CBDC) since 2014 — a sort of stablecoin, but run centrally, and carrying what was legally official currency. Of course, "working on" is a somewhat squishy concept — but at the least, the PBOC research bureau had been writing papers on the subject. Wang Xin, director of the research bureau, said on 8 July 2019 that the PBOC was paying "high attention" to Libra — and had accelerated its own official digital currency efforts as a direct response to Libra.[141] This became China's DC/EP (Digital Currency/ Electronic Payments) project.

Mu Changchun, then a deputy director-general of PBOC's Payment and Settlement Department, wrote in July 2019 that Libra would need central bank supervision — since it would have to act like a central bank, even as it disclaimed the responsibilities of one. He also questioned the technical capabilities of Libra's software and design as presented in June.[142] As of 2020, Mu is heading the DC/EP project.

Mark Zuckerberg and David Marcus later talked up the threat of a Chinese digital currency as a reason for Western regulators to let Libra through.

## Facebook responds

David Marcus posted to Facebook on 3 July 2019, two weeks after the announcement, somewhat disconcerted at the reaction to Libra.[143] "As expected there are also some questions and a few misunderstandings." Much of this seemed to be a direct response to critiques from the Financial Times.[144]

Cryptocurrency fans were upset that Libra was not a decentralised, permissionless blockchain, like Bitcoin. Marcus maintained that "one hundred geographically distributed, industry-diverse organizations is quite decentralized." He emphasised that they did want to move Libra to a fully permissionless system in due course.

Marcus' plan for financial inclusion was: "With Libra, anyone with a $40 smartphone and connectivity will have the ability to securely safeguard their assets, access the world economy, transact at a much lower cost, and over time access a whole range of financial services." He still didn't provide an actual mechanism for how this would work.

Marcus said that Facebook was working with regulators. He downplayed the notion that Facebook would have a controlling influence over the eventual network — so you wouldn't have to trust Facebook itself too much.

## Did Facebook have any idea what it was doing?

Facebook proposed a system that was clearly meant to be *big*. They're big enough to affect the world, and they set out big plans.

Not only did Facebook not talk to regulators early on — Libra's creators seemed unaware of recent financial history. They didn't research the history of their proposed reserve model, and didn't realise they'd come up with precisely the sort of shadow banking that made the 2008 financial crisis blow up really badly.

Sheila Bair, former chair of the Federal Deposit Insurance Corporation (FDIC) — who guarantee bank deposits up to $100,000 in the US — described the problem in early July:[145]

> Libra proposes the failed business model used by money market funds prior to the financial crisis. It wants you to buy Libra on the promise that the coin will maintain stable value, but there will be no regulatory oversight of what Libra actually does with your money and no capital and liquidity requirements that you would typically find with a bank.

> That structure proved disastrous during the 2008 crisis, when the Reserve Fund, a money market fund that heavily invested in Lehman Bros debt, "broke the buck" and prompted widespread runs on other money market funds.

Bair suggested the Federal Reserve Board should regulate Libra's reserve — as it does banks.

Did Facebook hire anyone who'd worked at a central bank, or for a government, on serious macroeconomics — someone who could talk to regulators in their own language — at any point since Morgan Beller started looking into cryptocurrencies for them in 2017?

Well, no — in June 2019, David Marcus said that "we need someone who knows how economies tend to work, who understands how to operate in a very complex, decentralized governance type of environment."[146]

You might think "someone who knows how economies tend to work" would have been a useful sort of person to have on the team *before* the big announcement. Presumably, Christian Catalini was the wrong sort of economist.

Marcus' appearances before the US House and Senate in July did not alleviate these concerns. Libra was not just a financial product, and Facebook was not just untrustworthy — Libra was Facebook expressing power. But worse than that — would Libra be *incompetent* power?

# Chapter 10:
# David Marcus before the US House and Senate

> Governments won't let Facebook use its superpower — negligence — to disrupt their economy. Enabling genocide in Myanmar is one thing, but messing with our ability to buy Chick-fil-A and Land Rovers is another level.
>
> — Scott Galloway, NYU Stern[147]

On 16 and 17 July, the United States Congress called Facebook to account for its plans for the world's money.

The governments of the US and the European Union are great fans of business — they want *you* to go out and make a great big pile of money. Many of the legislators at the July hearings loved the innovation of Libra — and they loved what Facebook was promising with Libra.

But governments worry when a big new player doesn't seem to know what it's talking about, and won't acknowledge the incredibly obvious implications of its plans. Did Facebook even understand what followed from what it was saying?

In an era of rancorous distrust throughout United States politics, Libra brought forth a groundswell of bipartisan agreement: Republicans and Democrats both hated the Libra plan, and everything about it, the moment they saw it.

David Marcus appeared as head of Facebook's Calibra unit, and a founder of the Libra project. He spoke precisely and earnestly in detail, wanting to give legislators the best possible impression of a project he cared about deeply.

But Libra's biggest problem was Facebook. Even if Libra had been a good idea — which the legislators weren't convinced of — Facebook was flatly unacceptable as Libra's creator and sponsor. These hearings were not just about Libra — they covered all of Facebook's other bad behaviour over the previous few years.

Looking back, the July 2019 hearings dealt the mortal blow to the original Libra plan. Everything after this was the hot air slowly wheezing out.

# Lost in the inbox

The US government first got wind of Facebook's private currency plan in early 2019. The Senate Committee on Banking, Housing, and Urban Affairs sent a letter to Mark Zuckerberg on 9 May, signed by Mike Crapo (R-ID) and Sherrod Brown (D-OH), asking for more detail about the project[148] — particularly how Facebook would protect consumer financial data.[*]

The Committee didn't have a reply from Facebook by the time of the 18 June announcement of Libra. On 19 June, the Committee called Facebook to appear before them for a 16 July hearing.[149] Facebook didn't answer the letter until 8 July[113] — a week before the hearing.

Just a few hours after Facebook announced Libra, Maxine Waters (D, CA-43), chair of the House Committee on Financial Services, had asked Facebook to halt the project while legislators examined it. Patrick McHenry (R, NC-10), the top Republican on the committee, asked Waters to hold a House hearing about Libra. This was scheduled for 17 July.[150]

# Facebook's trust deficit

One Congressional official told the Financial Times: "Facebook thought they could hide behind the fact that there are twenty-seven other partners in Libra. But members know that this is Facebook's project, and this is a chance to go after them for things like Cambridge Analytica."[151]

After Senator Crapo opened the Senate hearing, Senator Brown spoke:

> Facebook is dangerous. Now, Facebook might not intend to be dangerous — but surely, they don't respect the power of the technologies they are playing with — like a toddler who has gotten his hands on a book of matches. Facebook has burned down the house over and over, and called every arson a learning experience … The last thing that we need is to concentrate even more power. It would be crazy to give them a chance to experiment with bank accounts, to use powerful tools they don't understand.

---

[*]    Senators' affiliations are given by party (Republican or Democrat) and state. Representatives' affiliations also include their district.

Nine of the seventeen senators who asked questions at the hearing distrusted Facebook in particular, and didn't trust Marcus' promises that Facebook's Calibra unit would keep users' spending data isolated from the main Facebook platform — after all the times Facebook had broken previous privacy promises, good and hard. The House was similarly skeptical.

Both the House and Senate seemed amazed at Facebook's effrontery — the company had come from a $5 billion Federal Trade Commission fine just a few days earlier, Senator Brown mentioned Facebook's role in the recent Myanmar genocide ... and here Facebook was presenting its own private currency for a virtual country of two billion people. Brown added:

> After people's data and private messages have been stolen and sold, after you've let Russian bots try to throw the 2016 election — with no contrition, I might add — after you've abetted genocide in foreign countries, you really think people should trust you with their bank accounts and our economy? I think that's delusional.

Even if Libra was a good idea, Facebook was the wrong company to be putting it forward. Brian Schatz (D-HI) said: "You're making an argument for cryptocurrency generally. The question is not, should the United States lead in this area — the question is: why Facebook? And why before you've fixed your other stuff."

Brad Sherman (D, CA-30) said: "Madam Chair, we need to get Mark Zuckerberg here. This is the biggest thing, or it tries to be the biggest thing, this committee will deal with this decade. And while we have one of his employees here, this is Zuckerberg's program."

## The platypus of money

Rep. McHenry opened by asking: "Mr. Marcus, I've read your white paper. I understand the nature of digital currency and digital technology. What is a Libra? ... Is it a security? Is it a commodity? Is it an exchange-traded fund?"

Marcus said that Libra was a digital currency, to be used as a payment tool — but several other legislators echoed McHenry's confusion.

Libra was promoted as being an everyday currency — but it would work very like an exchange-traded fund.

This question was important: "If it's 'none of the above' in our current regulatory structure," asked McHenry, "how do you comply with regulations?" Bill Huizenga (R, MI-02), who had worked on crypto-asset regulation, said, "What is this, fish or fowl? And it seems that it's more of a platypus to me, that it evolves in its different parts."

Jim Himes (D, CT-04) was blunter: "You said this is not an exchange-traded fund. I'm a former banker. Looks to me exactly like an exchange-traded fund, backed by short-term instruments and foreign currency. It has a creation and remittance mechanism. So elaborate for me why this is not an exchange-traded fund."

Marcus detailed Calibra's FinCEN and state registrations for McHenry, and said that Libra was working with the G7 Working Group on Stablecoins and with FINMA, the Swiss regulator. To Himes, he admitted that the mechanism was similar to an ETF — but that Libra tokens were not an investment with an expectation of profit.

Himes was not satisfied: "Users will have the profoundly unfamiliar experience of assuming foreign currency risk ... How will you make transparent what you acknowledged is foreign currency risk that consumers will face?" Marcus responded that the Calibra wallet would include "education."

## Consumer protection

Consumers use money — but they mostly don't understand the financial system. Most people have a bank account hooked to a card; a lot of people without bank accounts have a prepaid card that can be topped up. A service like PayPal looks a lot like a current account at a bank — you have an account, you have money sitting in it, you can buy things with it.

Libra would look like banking to those people — especially when Facebook promoted it by saying things like "banking the unbanked."

Joyce Beatty (D, OH-03) was chair of the subcommittee on diversity and inclusion, and this was her particular area:

> Are you taking people's money and letting them pay for things, letting them transfer money? ... We know those who are unbanked or underbanked are that for a reason. This is very complicated. ... How do you take somebody from my district who is underbanked or unbanked, and educate them? No financial literacy. They think you're a

bank because even when you mention PayPal and those systems which you were the president of, I used PayPal as a store owner but it was tied to my credit card, it was tied to the regulations of the federal government. So, how do you tell us that it's not banking?

Jim Tester (D-MT) worried about security of deposits — "In 2008 there was a run on banks, and a number of companies that went belly up. Nobody anticipated there would be a run. Nobody."

Kyrsten Sinema (D-AZ) worried about ordinary people being ripped off by malicious actors on the Libra blockchain:

> Your head of product, Kevin Weil, told TechCrunch on June 18th[152] that there are "no plans for the Libra Association to take a role in actively vetting" developers of wallets, exchanges, or other related apps. But failing to vet developers would expose Arizonans to scammers, which is unacceptable.
>
> … Let's say an unsavory app developer that's based in Pakistan utilizes an exchange that's based in Thailand to rip off an Arizonan who's using a wallet that was built in Spain, so they steal all of their Libra. And that, of course, is minted by an association based in Switzerland. So which law enforcement or government or agency in which country does the Arizonan call to seek his or her Libra and financial recourse in this situation?

Marcus said that there would be full protection for Calibra Wallet users — but if they insisted on using a non-US wallet, "it will be the role of the Libra Association to ensure that there will be proper education so that consumers can make informed choices."

Marcus' pitch to education didn't convince. Ed Perlmutter (D, CO-07) said:

> We all have the same question for you, and that's the resistance you're feeling, because we think you're a bank but you're not quite like a bank, and if you're a bank, we regulate the heck out of ya, because we have seen a lot of people lose money where there hasn't been regulations. So that's the resistance that I feel. I want to support your innovation, I want to support the efficiency you people believe you're bringing to the table, but I also don't want anybody getting hurt here.

# Good intentions are not enough

It was glaringly obvious that a new currency at Facebook scale would be a systemic risk — it would be big enough to break everything.

Regulators and legislators had Libra's number immediately — they knew this kind of foolishness, and they knew that these Bitcoin venture capital bros were absolutely stupid and arrogant enough to do another 2008 financial crisis all by themselves.

Marcus was faced with defending the plans for Libra, when the plans barely existed as yet. All he could do was restate Facebook's good intentions.

Gregory Meeks (D, NY-05), Chair of the Subcommittee on Consumer Protections and Financial Institutions, set out the problem:

> I can say with confidence that Lehman Bros, Bear Stearns and the entire subprime mortgage ecosystem did not set out to bring the global financial system to its knees. I can say with confidence that the legitimately brilliant minds and Nobel Prize winners, in fact, behind LTCM [*Long-Term Capital Management*] did not set out to trigger the Asian financial crises, but they nearly broke the global markets. And I can also say with confidence that the deregulation of the early 1980s and bankers did not set out to trigger the savings and loans crisis, but it did.
>
> Not only that, they all typically founded their logic in innovation, expanding access to financial services, and arguments of inclusion. And yet, they all broke the system. And the people at the bottom of the socioeconomic ladder systemically paid the heaviest price. So you may be speaking earnestly when you tell us the lofty goals, but I was here in Congress when Secretary Paulson came to us and told us we were within days of a complete shutdown of the global financial system. I don't expect you to understand what that was like — but I assure you, it was absolutely terrifying, and one of my worst moments in Congress.

Meeks, Nydia Velázquez (D, NY-07) and Barry Loudermilk (R, GA-14) suggested that Libra be designated "systemically important," which would mean enhanced oversight of Libra by the Financial

Stability Oversight Council (FSOC). Marcus said that Libra had been talking to FSOC.

Carolyn Maloney (D, NY-12), Chair for the Subcommittee on Investor Protection, asked: "Will you commit to doing a small pilot program for Libra, first limited to no more than one million users and overseen by the Federal Reserve and the SEC?"

In the payments world, small pilot programmes for new ventures are routine. This is the standard way of doing a new thing — because you never know quite what will happen, and the weird things people will do, until you go live. PayPal ran several such pilots when Marcus was there.

And yet, Marcus wouldn't commit to a small pilot — even though it would be completely ordinary to just start small to see what happened, like every other new payment initiative does. Maloney asked for this repeatedly — "The Libra reserve could be managing too much money, which could make it systemic; too much money could be pulled out of banks in order to buy Libra" — but Marcus just would not agree to launching Libra with an initial pilot program, in the normal way.

Michael San Nicolas (D, Guam; vice-chair, House Committee on Financial Services) asked a simple and obvious question: "What does the organization project the average user will have as a Libra balance?" Marcus had no answer: "We have not projected average balances at this point." Marcus couldn't give even an estimate of how much money Facebook expected Libra users to be holding in the system.

San Nicolas hit the roof. "Do you really expect me to believe that? Facebook is built around average users, average number of hits. Visa, Mastercard, all these huge players are signing up, and you guys have no idea how much you expect to have in an average Libra account?" He flatly refused to believe that large corporations would sign up as Libra Association members without any idea of the numbers.

San Nicolas pointed out the obvious: that the working float in the Libra system would be in the hundreds of billions of dollars, at least — and that this would be enough to affect the US dollar. If Libra was allowed to launch at that scale, stopping or regulating Libra would be politically impossible — no matter the risks.

# Libra, money laundering and sanctions

Even the most innovation-loving and deregulation-minded legislators were worried about money laundering risks and international sanctions — where the US has tremendous power to levy sanctions, since it controls the dollar.

Making international payments easy was key to Libra's pitch. If there was any way for bad actors to use Libra to get around anti-money-laundering (AML) rules, they would — Ann Wagner (R, MN-02) worried that "North Korea uses cryptocurrencies to get around our sanctions all the time." Would the Libra Association blacklist addresses if requested?

Rather than answering directly, Marcus kept responding to sanctions enforcement questions with a pitch to patriotism. "If we don't lead in this space, others will." If Libra didn't do a coin, some other (unnamed) persons would do one, "out of reach from our national security apparatus." He meant China, and its moves to a digital yuan — moves that China had accelerated in direct response to the Libra announcement.

Marcus did add that the Libra Association would register with FinCEN, and that all wallets operating in the US would be strongly compliant — though he didn't mention wallets outside the US.

Roger Williams (R, TX-25) asked about the white paper statement that users would be pseudonymous on the Libra blockchain, and might have multiple addresses. Marcus said that the issue was that adding personal information to a blockchain would be irresponsible, but the on-ramps and off-ramps would be regulated — though this didn't address anyone who accessed the Libra blockchain directly.

Bill Foster (D, IL-11) was particularly concerned with direct users of the Libra blockchain. "Once a large fraction of Libra would be transferred into self-custody, and then there starts to be a significant flow amongst the self-custody entities out on the dark web or other places, how do you prevent that from actually allowing things like ransomware? ... So if there's one wallet out in some set of islands or something like this, that doesn't follow US ... are we just out of luck there, and all the illicit transactions will flow through there?"

French Hill (R, AR-02) asked about Libra and international remittances and Know-Your-Customer (KYC) rules, which are part of enforcing AML. Marcus assured him that the Calibra wallet would be strongly compliant — but outside of the US, Libra would be taking a "country-by-country approach."

Rep. McHenry pointed out that if Libra successfully decentralised and went permissionless, AML would be impossible by design. Remember that the entire point of permissionless decentralisation in crypto was to be beyond any possible government control of transactions. Marcus claimed that even with a decentralised Libra, the Libra Association would "likely" still run most of the processing nodes for the Libra blockchain.

## What's in it for Facebook?

It was entirely unclear how Facebook would make money from Libra — how they'd get a return on their not-inconsiderable investment, without charging fees or exploiting personal data.

Libra Association members (at least) could buy Libra Investment Tokens, which would pay a dividend from profits on the Libra reserve — which seemed odd for a nonprofit association. Patrick Toomey (R-PA) asked, "Could you explain how paying potentially unlimited dividends to investors is not a for-profit operation?" Marcus said that dividends would not be unlimited, and that Facebook was discussing this with the G7 Working Group on Stablecoins.

The closest Marcus could get to stating a business case for Libra was that easier payments would mean that "ninety million businesses" on Facebook platforms would expand, and this would give them more money to buy ads. He also suggested that Calibra might offer financial services in the future — in partnership with financial institutions, as Calibra was not going to get into banking.

Sylvia Garcia (D, TX-29) tried and failed to get even a rough estimate from Marcus of what Facebook had spent on Libra to date — on all the funding and all the engineering. TechCrunch had asked Facebook this question two weeks previously — so it's a number the company should have been able to give a rough value for, by the time of the hearing.[153]

## The Libra Association

Marcus stated repeatedly that Facebook was just one Association member, and they wouldn't and couldn't control it "We don't want to control the network, and we think it's important that those decisions are made collegially with the other cofounding members."

Legislators didn't buy this one at all. Senator Brown said, "You know that only Facebook has access to two billion people, and to say that you are just one of many is simply not true."

Lacy Clay (D, MO-01) pointed out the obvious conflict of interest: the Libra reserve promised stability, and that the Libra currency would be backed one-to-one — but all the incentives were for the Association to manage the reserve for maximum profit, like any other investment portfolio.

Several noted that Facebook seemed to have chosen all the Association members to maintain its own control, and Anthony Gonzalez (R, OH-16) said: "there's something glaringly missing from the group, which are everyday users" — there was no mechanism for Libra's users to influence the Association.

Rashida Tlaib (D, MI-13) asked: "Can a member of the Libra Association — the group of friends — be voted out by Libra users?" Marcus said that "the way that governance will evolve will allow for that in the future."

Tlaib also worried how connected the Association members were to Facebook — the overlapping board memberships and investment relationships.

Senator Schatz had spoken to other prospective Association members:

> What I'm hearing — and they're terrified to talk about this publicly — is that members of the consortium actually have lots of questions too, similar to the questions that are being offered on this dais, and they have great reservations about moving forward — but they don't want to be left out because of Facebook's market power.

Jesús "Chuy" García (D, IL-04) said: "Facebook's voice is more like the Godfather's voice in the Family. It's true that it's just one voice among many — but, you know, it's also the only voice that matters."

## Switzerland

Several legislators were unhappy that the Libra Association was being founded outside the US. Why Switzerland? What was wrong with the US?

In his answer to Mike Rounds (R-SD), Marcus tried to have it both ways:

> We believe that a global digitally native currency that will be used by people all around the world would benefit from being headquartered in an international place that is

also the home of many respected international organizations … The reality, though, if you look at the current composition of the Libra Association members, those are mostly American companies.

Some didn't buy this — Senator Brown spoke of Facebook wanting to "run their own currency out of a Swiss bank account," and others spoke of how hard it would be to make US regulation and consumer protection reach as far as a Swiss nonprofit.

Some pro-blockchain representatives brought up a lack of regulatory clarity in the US — crypto-assets are under multiple US legal frameworks. A few members asked Marcus if the Libra Association had been set up in Switzerland to take advantage of that country's clearer regulation of cryptos. Marcus said to Bryan Steil (R, WI-01) that "the clarity of regulation was definitely one of the factors for Switzerland, but one out of many. I do think we would have had the ability from a regulatory framework to do this in the United States."

## Censorship of payments

Several Republicans brought up the possibility of payment censorship, if Libra was subject to Facebook's rules on behaviour. Some right-wing media figures had been banned from Facebook for breaching its terms of service — Sean Duffy (R, WI 07) mentioned alt-right figure Milo Yiannopoulos and Nation of Islam leader Louis Farrakhan.

Duffy pulled out a twenty-dollar bill, and said how "everybody can use a twenty-dollar bill, this twenty-dollar bill doesn't discriminate on anything." He asked if Libra would be as free to use as the twenty-dollar bill.

Marcus said that Facebook did not want to tell people what to do with their money, but that they would need to be "very thoughtful" about this. Duffy said that the "thoughtful answer" would be: "I'm going to behave like a fiat currency — if you abide by the law, you have access."

## Innovation and blockchain

Several in attendance were enthusiastic about Libra — even just as an example of the sort of innovation that should be encouraged. Others were fans of blockchains and cryptocurrency in particular.

Rep. McHenry said at the end of the House session:

I don't know how history's going to judge this hearing. I fear not well, though … there is this underlying fear amongst policy makers here on the Hill, because they don't understand cryptocurrency and digital assets. That's my fear, that this will not wear well historically — the concerns raised, the questions raised. … I hope there won't be much that is laughed at in 30 years. My fears, however, are that the reactionary element that was brought up here today in part will be dealt with with great disdain after the next generation of internet technology.

## Whoops!

In his written statement to the Senate,[154] Marcus said that "for the purposes of data and privacy protections, the Swiss Federal Data Protection and Information Commissioner (FDPIC) will be the Libra Association's privacy regulator." The FDPIC promptly told CNBC: "Until today we have not been contacted by the promoters of Libra."[155] The FDPIC contacted Facebook and gave them until the end of August to give them the information they would need.[156]

(Mark Zuckerberg followed up on this in his October testimony to the House: "The misunderstanding there was that I believe that he and the team had been working with the primary Swiss financial regulator, FINMA, and now we are also working with the data regulator.")

Less than an hour after Marcus denied to Rep. Velázquez that Libra would attempt to be a bank — "The Libra Association or Calibra have no plans in engaging in banking activities" — the official Libra Twitter tweeted a 26 June Wall Street Journal article, with the text: "By creating a de facto central bank, Libra could succeed where other cryptocurrencies fall short," which was the subheading of the Journal article.[157] The tweet was deleted almost immediately — but not before others saved screenshots of it.[158]

## Outside experts weigh in

Five outside witnesses appeared at the House hearing — Professor Chris Brummer of Georgetown University Law Center (who has commented extensively on Libra), Prof. Katharina Pistor of Columbia Law School, Robert Weissman of Public Citizen, Prof.

Gary Gensler of MIT (who was previously Chairman of the CFTC), and Meltem Demirors of CoinShares, a long-time cryptocurrency advocate.[159]

## Chris Brummer

Prof. Brummer focused on the Libra white paper — and how it completely failed to disclose the risks of Libra for consumers.[160]

If a currency in the reserve basket dropped in value, using Libra would expose ordinary users to foreign exchange risk — and the white paper didn't even list the particular currencies that would be in the basket.

There could even be panic-induced runs on Libra if there was trouble at Facebook, at another Libra Association member, or at an authorized reseller — or if there was a hack on the Calibra wallet, or a hack on a popular app built on the Libra platform.

Facebook's governance plans for the Libra Association were obscure. Facebook claimed the goal of the reserve was "value preservation" — but all the incentives were to work the reserve as hard as possible for profit. "Perhaps the most problematic aspect of the White Paper's disclosure is its failure to clearly disclose that holders of Libra are exposed to counterparty risk in the form of mismanagement of reserve investments."

Libra couldn't possibly comply with money laundering or international sanctions rules by regulating only the resellers, and not the network itself — one reseller in a lax jurisdiction could compromise the whole system. The Libra Association itself would need financial intelligence units (FIUs), around the world — the same way that banks and other financial institutions need FIUs. "Otherwise, users of Libra coins could well find themselves answering questions by law enforcement officials in the wake of what they thought were ordinary Libra purchases … Ultimately, the weakest link in the network can become a gateway for all kinds of wrongdoers."

Brummer noted the explicit statement in the white paper that the Libra blockchain would allow users to control one or more addresses not linked to their real-world identity — and how this flouted the Bank Secrecy Act travel rule, which requires information such as the name and address of the sender. Prof. Gensler interjected to note that "there is not currently a way that you could actually foreclose somebody on the sanctions list from getting this coin and transacting," unless you listed the addresses of sanctioned entities in the Libra network software itself.

It wasn't clear whether Libra currency tokens would be securities under US law. Libra Investment Tokens — which were still in the white paper at this time — certainly would be. The Libra reserve plan very closely resembled money market funds and exchange-traded funds, and would almost certainly qualify in the US as an investment company under the Investment Company Act of 1940.

## Katharina Pistor

Prof. Pistor described Libra as a for-profit currency of currencies — it was built to make money for its members from interest on the reserve.[161] The Libra Association's legal structure meant it wasn't meaningfully accountable to anyone — not to Libra holders, nor to the governments responsible for the safe assets is the Libra reserve.

US legal frameworks leave plenty of room for regulatory arbitrage — moving jurisdictions while still being able to wield your financial force. Pistor considered it unlikely that Libra, as described in the white papers, could be effectively regulated at all.

Libra would only be as stable as the public reserves of government-managed currencies it rested upon — "free riding on a public safety net for which they are not paying." Rep. Velázquez asked Pistor about runs on the Libra — Pistor answered that the US would likely have to backstop "any uncertainties or run on the Libra, even if it emanates from elsewhere in the world."

Libra would likely be large enough to be a systemic risk if it failed. Since the 2008 financial crisis, regulators have required banks to have plans to unwind the organisation in an orderly manner in case of insolvency. They would have to require the same of Libra.

Pistor noted that the very safe assets the Libra plan rested upon were already in high demand. If Libra was successful, the Association might have trouble finding sufficient safe assets.

Worse yet, the finance industry might synthesise "safe" assets to meet the demand, as they did in the lead-up to the 2008 crisis. When house prices went down, these "safe" assets turned toxic overnight. "Libra has the potential to transition in no time from 'too small to care' to 'too big to fail,'" Pistor said.

A global currency would require an extensive personal identification infrastructure, or it couldn't meet AML requirements — which is what the digital identity proposal in the Libra white paper was about. "Facebook might become *the* provider of a global digital identity. The question before us is not whether such identities need to be created, but who shall do so — governments that are subject to democratic control, or private actors that can insulate themselves from any accountability."

## Robert Weissman

On 2 July, thirty-three nonprofits, including Public Citizen, wrote to the US House and Senate committees and US regulators with a list of concerns about Libra — on governance, national sovereignty, law enforcement, tax policy, consumer protection, privacy, competition and systemic risk. "All of us believe the risks posed by Facebook's proposal are too great to allow the plan to proceed with so many unanswered questions."[162] The testimony of Robert Weissman of Public Citizen built upon the letter.[163]

Libra would let Facebook turn social media market dominance into financial market dominance — and then dominance of commerce itself. Calibra would let Facebook dominate Libra in practice, even as it had only one vote in the Association.

Runs on Libra were trivially possible — for instance, competition between currencies in the Libra basket, such as users selling euros for Libra then buying dollars. "It is entirely possible the Association would not be able to pay out." A currency might crash, or a "safe" reserve asset might go bad — leaving Libra no longer fully backed.

Rep. Clay asked Weissman about systemic risks if a majority of US Facebook users became Libra users. Weissman described how a run on Libra could require government action on the scale of the Troubled Asset Relief Program in the 2008 financial crisis — which disbursed $431 billion to prop up distressed shadow banks.

Unless Libra tokens were legally defined as "money," a lot of US consumer protection laws would not in fact apply. Jurisdiction over international transactions was unclear — if you bought something overseas and you were scammed, what could you do about it? Would the Libra Association protect Libra users? Weissman said that Libra would become "a haven for hucksters":

> Altogether, the world would be looking at a system of the old Swiss banking secrecy rules, or Cayman Island secrecy on steroids — with not just secret banks, but secret transactions across borders into secret banks, or into secret non-bank corporations that may exist only virtually.

Weissman described the anticompetitive power of Libra: "No other company can do what Facebook can do and suddenly magically make appear this new product inside your phone, inside your life, inside your mind, for two billion people."

Weissman said that Facebook "has demonstrated that its policies and statements are snapshots in time rather than real, abiding commitments and guarantees to consumers and the public." It had repeatedly failed to keep even to its voluntary commitments. "In short, this is not a corporation that should get the benefit of the doubt."

## Gary Gensler

Prof. Gensler, who led the CFTC from 2009 to 2014, was more positive about the Libra project — he thought Libra "may help spur greater competition in payments, potentially enhancing access and reducing costs."[164]

But he warned that the Libra reserve should be regulated by the SEC per the Investment Company Act of 1940 as a pooled investment in foreign currencies, and the Libra Association should be registered as an investment advisor.

There would be two classes of investors in Libra — the holders of Libra Investment Tokens, who got a dividend, and the holders of Libra currency tokens, who got no dividend or interest, and just had risks. The two would have conflicting interests.

Alternately, the Libra reserve could be regulated like a bank — since it would function as one, in issuing its own private electronic banknotes.

Gensler also noted the systemic risk issues that money market funds caused in the 2008 financial crisis — and that there would need to be clear restrictions on how the Libra reserve managed its assets.

Rep. Velázquez asked Gensler why Libra was being founded in Switzerland rather than the US. He answered:

> You could have a nonprofit and yet still pay dividends, which is kind of foreign to the way we think here. I think it is also a signaling effect to all of their users that they are less controlled by the US, and when this Libra reserve gets big at some point in time, if any developed country is going to use the Libra instead of the US dollar and Libraize instead of dollarize, I think it signals in the

future: hey, we're not under the control of whatever future US president and sanctions regime.

## Meltem Demirors

Demirors has long worked in cryptocurrency advocacy. Demirors' main point was that Libra should not be compared to Bitcoin — Bitcoin was a public network, but Libra was a private enterprise built by and for a large company.[165] She pitched for looser regulations on Bitcoin companies.

Rep. McHenry asked Demirors about cryptocurrency in general, and the challenges for the industry. Demirors described the problems with inconsistent regulation, and used Switzerland as an example of a country where crypto regulation was clearer.

McHenry asked Demirors' position on Libra. "Facebook should be allowed to innovate just as anyone else in this country is allowed to innovate," she answered, "but it should not be allowed to pursue this path under the guise of being an open cryptocurrency like Bitcoin."

After the outside witnesses, Chairwoman Waters concluded the hearing, and thanked and led a round of applause for the witnesses. She finished: "No corporation this big or this powerful works as a nonprofit without making a lot of money … we should have more hearings and get Mr. Zuckerberg here himself. I'm with that."

# Chapter 11:
# July to September 2019:
# Libra runs the gauntlet

I think there's a number of very constructive feedback coming from many of the regulators and the technical staff, from central banks to institutions like the SEC and others, and it's been extremely helpful.

— Christian Catalini[82]

Things didn't go any better for the Libra project after the Senate and House hearings. The regulators were still unhappy, the central banks were still working on responding to this obvious threat to economic stability, and the public still didn't understand what Libra was, or why they'd want to start using a whole new currency.

## Refreshing the White Papers

Facebook quietly updated the various white papers after the Senate and House hearings — most notably removing all mention of Libra Investment Tokens in the 23 July versions, and replacing it with "the distribution of incentives in the form of Libra to qualifying Founding Members per the Incentives Distribution Policy." The incentive policy wasn't set out.[166]

The main white paper went through eight versions from June 2019 to February 2020, mostly updating Libra Association membership as prospective members dropped out. The Libra Association white paper changed the word "investors" to "members" between July and August.[167]

## Switzerland on stablecoins

Libra wanted to set up shop in Switzerland — so it absolutely needed to be square with the Swiss regulator, the Financial Markets Authority (FINMA). Libra contacted FINMA to ask about the legal status of their planned coin, and apply for a licence as a payment system.

You might think they'd have done that *before* announcing their project to the world, including their plans to set up in Switzerland — but better late than never.

FINMA published their guidance on stablecoins on 11 September 2019.[168] This was a supplement to FINMA's existing guidance on ICO tokens and related crypto-assets — such as existing projects that already called themselves "stablecoins."

If Libra wanted to run a basket-based coin, the Libra reserve would be regulated as a collective investment scheme — and the users' money would be regulated in Switzerland like bank deposits were. If Libra ran coins based on national currencies, the purchasers' money would also be regulated like bank deposits.

FINMA had found previously that a token might need to be registered as *all of* a bank, a security (an investment scheme) and a payment system with anti-money-laundering obligations.

Stablecoins pegged to a national currency at a fixed redemption rate — *e.g.*, one token for one Swiss franc — would be regulated as bank deposits, and the issuer would need to be licensed as a bank.

When a claim to redeem a token could depend on market prices — say, when the token is pegged to a basket of currencies — all risks had to be borne by the issuer, or the token itself would be a collective investment scheme. If a token was not redeemable directly with the issuer — such as Libra, which could only be redeemed via Libra Authorized Resellers — this could trigger a requirement for licensing under other rules, such as the Financial Market Infrastructure Act, which protects against systemic risks from derivatives (analogous to Dodd-Frank in the US).

The guidance also included a list of questions for aspiring stablecoin issuers — the issuer would need to answer how the value of the coin was calculated, how a basket-based coin worked, and how to redeem coins.

FINMA noted that "the highest international anti-money laundering standards would need to be ensured throughout the entire ecosystem of the project" — and that Libra in particular required an "internationally coordinated approach."

All of this would make Libra into a system for well-documented users in highly-regulated rich countries — and not so available in poorer countries, with billions of under-documented people.

Mark Branson, Director of FINMA, was interviewed by Neue Zürcher Zeitung about Libra on 12 September, the day after the stablecoin guidance came out. Swiss politicians had worried that Libra could be a risk to Switzerland's reputation — but Branson said that FINMA could mitigate that risk with credible regulation, supervision and frameworks. But Switzerland couldn't do it on their own — "a project of such global dimensions can only be addressed through international coordination and consultation with other regulators."[169]

Branson wasn't worried by Libra — he said in October, "I am much more nervous about projects which develop in a dark corner in the financial system somewhere, spread themselves out through cyberspace and one day are too big to be stopped."[170]

Swiss National Bank chairman Thomas Jordan spoke on 5 September on "Currencies, money and digital tokens" — "as long as prices, wages and loans are set in Swiss francs, the SNB can influence incentives for savers and borrowers via its monetary policy and thus ensure price stability over the medium term. However, if stablecoins pegged to foreign currencies were to establish themselves in Switzerland, the effectiveness of our monetary policy could be impaired."[171]

The Federal Council, the head of government of Switzerland, followed with a press release in October: "The Federal Council is keeping a very close eye on global stablecoin projects and their associated opportunities and risks."[172]

# Other regulators

## European Union

In mid-August, the European Commission started an antitrust investigation into Libra, and sent questionnaires to prospective Association members saying that they were "currently investigating potential anti-competitive behavior." The Commission also wanted to look into the governance structure of the Libra Association, and Facebook's plans to integrate Libra into WhatsApp and Messenger.[173]

Yves Mersch of the European Central Bank spoke on 2 September at the ECB Legal Conference. Mersch considered Libra to be unusually risky even for a private currency: "I sincerely hope that the people of Europe will not be tempted to leave behind the safety and soundness of established payment solutions and channels in favour of the beguiling but treacherous promises of Facebook's siren call."[174]

Facebook insisted in September that it had been working with regulatory authorities in Europe. French cryptocurrency journalist

Grégory Raymond discovered otherwise: "According to my information, the French authorities have not received an application for accreditation from Libra (needed to operate in the EU). To their knowledge, it's the same elsewhere in the EU: 'In the face of the risks identified, Facebook has so far provided no response to public authorities.'"[175]

Valdis Dombrovskis, the European Union financial services commissioner, sent Facebook a questionnaire in late September about money laundering, the financial stability of Libra reserves, and the privacy of its users' data.[176] Dombrovskis wanted to know how to regulate Libra-like coins in Europe — and if Libra should even be allowed to operate in the EU.[177]

## United Kingdom

Mark Carney, Governor of the Bank of England, discussed Libra in his August 2019 speech at the Jackson Hole Economic Symposium.[178] Libra was a "high profile" new entrant into payments, and "depending on its design, it could have substantial implications for both monetary and financial stability."

Carney worried about over-reliance on the US dollar. The US accounts for 10% of global trade and 15% of global GDP — but half of trade invoices and two-thirds of global securities are priced in dollars. Whenever the US economy is out of step with the rest of the world, the Federal Reserve's interest rates don't work for economies outside the US. This weakens the US in turn.

The Libra proposal inspired Carney to suggest the bankers start a new basket-based international currency — a "Synthetic Hegemonic Currency … perhaps through a network of central bank digital currencies."

The Financial Times said that, given what a disaster Libra's launch had been, "we hear a lot of the participants at Jackson Hole were rather miffed as to why Carney mentioned Facebook's stable coin idea at all."[179]

## United States

Between June and October 2019, Facebook hired seven additional lobbying firms to talk to the US government about cryptocurrencies and finance issues.[180]

The SEC had still not determined whether Libra was a security by the time SEC chair Jay Clayton appeared before the House Financial Services Committee on September 24.[181]

Sigal Mandelker, the US Treasury Undersecretary of Terrorism and Financial Intelligence, met in Switzerland on 10 September with officials from FINMA and the Bank for International Settlements to discuss Libra and cryptocurrencies.

Mandelker said, "Whether it's Bitcoin, Ethereum, Libra, our message is the same to all of these companies: anti-money laundering and combating the financing of terrorism has to be built into your design from the get-go." She said that the cryptocurrency industry had put a lot of effort into developing the technology — but far too little into regulating the networks they were building.[182] "They will have to comply with US standards if they're going to survive."[183]

## Australia

On 31 July, the Australian Securities and Investments Commission's Emerging Threats and Harm Committee met to discuss "the potential disruption to Australian financial markets posed by the Libra crypto-asset and ecosystem" and its "many threats and risks, including the proliferation of scams based on Libra via mobile apps."

Facebook's Australian executives were unable to answer four regulators' technical questions on 9 July. A meeting in October between senior Australian officials and Facebook US executives left the regulators no happier.

Elizabeth Hampton of the Office of the Australian Information Commissioner (OAIC) emailed her fellow regulators: "If we don't get answers to these questions from the US-based team we will then need to consider whether formal powers are exercised where available."

A spokesman for the OAIC said in November: "We remain concerned that Facebook and Calibra have only made broad public statements about privacy, and they have not addressed the information handling practices that will be in place to secure and protect personal information."[184]

## Singapore

Ravi Menon, managing director of the Monetary Authority of Singapore, said in September that "the global regulatory community is coming around to the view that we need a broadly consistent approach. Some of the macro financial risks are actually global in nature. It's not as if one regulator can act on its own."

Menon was interested in the possible benefits of Libra — but said "the history of private money over the last three thousand years has not been a good one." Private issuers would have incentive to debase the currency — to just issue coins whenever it was profitable for the currency's proprietors.[185]

# Trusting Facebook with your privacy

Facebook's obvious use case for a payment system was to be yet another source of personal information on users. Every regulator and commentator noticed this immediately.

Calibra staff promised that Facebook would keep Calibra data separate from other Facebook data — though without any details, as Calibra's systems didn't exist yet.[186]

On 5 August, data protection officials from Albania, Australia, Burkina Faso, Canada, the EU, the UK and the USA wrote to Facebook, worried about Libra's privacy risks — particularly given Facebook's terrible track record with personal data.[187]

# Did consumers even want Libra?

It wasn't clear that consumers were even that interested in Libra. Brent Thill, a financial analyst at Jefferies, surveyed 600 US social media users in July. Eighty percent said they were unlikely to buy Libra — mainly because they didn't trust Facebook.[188]

The Libra plan brought to mind successful social media payment systems like WeChat Pay and Alipay in China. But in Europe, consumers already had good mobile payment systems — and the US was fast catching up.

The promise of better cross-border payments would appeal to some users — but this wouldn't be the mass market that Libra would need. Even then, it was unclear how Libra would make cross-border payments better while keeping proper regulation — Facebook seemed to assume that blockchain-based tokens had special qualities they didn't actually set out anywhere.

But the Libra project's biggest problem wasn't the end users — it was its own internal troubles. These boiled over in October.

# Chapter 12:
# October 2019:
# Libra's bad month

It was a neat idea that'll never happen, and I have nothing else to say about it.

— Jamie Dimon, JP Morgan Chase, on Libra,
18 October 2019[189]

Libra's issues came to a head in October — when regulators worked out how to deal with "global stablecoins," most of the payment companies left Libra, and Mark Zuckerberg failed to sell Congress on Facebook's bona fides. And what was left of the Libra Association formally launched.

## The payment processors leave

All the payment companies left the Libra Association before the official October launch, except PayU — and Facebook seemed blindsided by this.

From June through to October 2019, there wasn't much visible activity around the Association. The Swiss nonprofit association itself technically had no members other than Facebook, and Facebook was the only company paying for staff or development — the other members were just lending their names to the endeavour.

But all was not well in the background.

Regulatory scrutiny spooked at least three members as early as August — two considered cutting ties, and a third worried about public support for Libra attracting the wrong sort of attention. "I think it's going to be difficult for partners who want to be seen as in compliance to be out there supporting it," said one company representative.[190]

Prospective members started worrying when regulators and politicians around the world hammered on the theme of Libra as funding terrorists and criminals, and as a threat to the world financial system. PayPal thought Facebook hadn't really addressed the backlash, and wasn't happy with Facebook not having put in the work with regulators before the launch — "companies don't want that to bleed into their businesses," said one person close to the company.[191]

Facebook was frustrated in turn by its partners not coming to the party. But, as one of the members said, "Some of those conversations should have taken place before the launch, to understand how regulators would think about this, so there wasn't so much pushback."

Facebook set up a meeting for Association members in Washington DC on 3 October — but on 1 October, the Wall Street Journal reported that Visa, Mastercard and other members were planning to leave.[192]

David Marcus tweeted to deny the Wall Street Journal story: "The part of this article suggesting we weren't on top of, or didn't share detailed information about how to secure Libra and protect the network against illegal activity is categorically untrue; (worth calling BS)."[193] But other press — who had spoken to the members who were leaving — backed up the Journal's claims.

PayPal pulled out of the 3 October meeting, and announced it was leaving Libra on Friday 4 October, two days after Marcus' denial. The company deleted its original June press release about joining the Libra Association.[194]

The Libra project was defiant: "We're better off knowing about this lack of commitment now, rather than later," said Libra communications chief Dante Disparte.

On 8 October, US Senators Sherrod Brown and Brian Schatz wrote to Visa, MasterCard, and Stripe, warning them against signing up to Libra until Facebook could answer the many deep concerns over the project:[195]

> Facebook appears to want the benefits of engaging in financial activities without the responsibility of being regulated as a financial services company. Facebook is attempting to accomplish that objective by shifting the risks and the need to design new compliance regimes on to regulated members of the Libra Association like your companies. If you take this on, you can expect a high level of scrutiny from regulators not only on Libra-related payment activities, but on all payment activities.

On 11 October, five more members left together: payment providers Stripe, Visa, Mastercard and Mercado Pago, and auction site eBay.[196]

Ajay Banga, CEO of Mastercard, said later that he had pulled Mastercard out because he couldn't get a hard commitment that "key members" of the Association would "not do anything that is not fully compliant with local law" — such as basic due diligence and know-your-customer. "Every time you talked to the main proponents of Libra, I said 'Would you put that in writing?' They wouldn't."[197]

Banga didn't see how Libra would make its money. "When you don't understand how money gets made, it gets made in ways you don't like." And Libra's claims of "financial inclusion" didn't make any coherent sense to him.

Some of the companies who left the Libra project in early October said Facebook had underestimated the regulatory reaction — and had greatly oversold how committed other members were.[198]

Facebook's ongoing privacy scandals and antitrust investigations meant Libra was tainted by association — "Facebook has been a lightning rod," said one former member. Facebook had thought the launch would be a "tremendous rollout" — but they didn't understand how serious the former members' worries were.

Several companies said that the final straw had been when Mark Zuckerberg was called on 9 October to testify before Congress, and when the senators wrote to the payment companies. "Some companies' entire business models were publicly threatened by incredibly powerful senators," said one, "who threatened to subject them to higher levels of scrutiny if they even so much as had a Libra node on one of their servers."[199]

Senator Brown issued a statement on the payment companies leaving: "Large payment companies are wise to avoid legitimizing Facebook's private, global currency. Facebook is too big and too powerful, and it is unconscionable for financial companies to aid it in monopolizing our economic infrastructure. I trust others will see the wisdom of avoiding this ill-conceived undertaking."[200]

US Treasury Secretary Steve Mnuchin disputed that the senators' letter had been a threat to the payment companies — he thought it was just a "very clear" statement that Libra had to meet anti-money-laundering standards. "I think they realized that they're not ready, they're not up to par. And I assume some of the partners got concerned and dropped out until they meet those standards."[201]

Olaf Scholz, the German Finance Minister, was also pleased at the departures: "It's a good sign that important companies have withdrawn from this project. I see the project as a threat to the autonomy of states and to democratic governance in our society. We must ensure that the issuance of a currency remains a matter for states and not large private companies."[202]

Booking Holdings (Priceline) dropped out on 14 October, just before the first official meeting of the Libra Association. Booking didn't comment on its departure[203] — but a source told the Financial Times that "it was not a company that liked to be associated with controversy."[204]

David Marcus was sanguine. "Of course, it's not great news in the short term, but in a way it's liberating," he tweeted[205] He told a panel at the International Monetary Fund conference in Washington on 16 October: "It will take time for us to address all of the regulatory concerns that were raised and it's our duty and our responsibility to come with answers to all of these questions … I think once we've done this then I think we'll see more banks and traditional financial services firms join the effort."[206]

In the wake of almost all the payment processors leaving, analysts Moffett Nathanson wrote:[207]

> We believe Libra will fail without the involvement of the major payments players, as they bring essential, deep payments expertise, trusted payments brands, global acceptance and settlement networks, and relationships with every major financial institution, government, and regulatory body around the world.

That is — the precise list of things Facebook would need to get Libra off the ground.

## Regulator reactions

Bruno Le Maire, France's finance minister, wrote in the Financial Times on 17 October: "Facebook's Libra is a threat to national sovereignty."[208] Le Maire's solution was to innovate in payments and technology — but under the central banks. "Neither political nor monetary sovereignty can be shared with private interests."

Benoît Cœuré of the European Central Bank said in October: "There is certainly no judgement that stablecoins shouldn't exist. In the case of Europe, neither the Commission nor the ECB intend to make Europe a no-fly zone for stablecoins. But when we talk about people's money, there is no trade-off between innovation and safety."[209]

Cœuré worried about smaller and developing countries — they might get cheaper and faster payments, but they risked "stablecoinisation."

The Financial Action Task Force (FATF), the international money laundering and terrorist financing watchdog, said on 18 October that stablecoins would be subject to the same rules as cryptocurrencies and traditional assets, and worried about "new risks regarding money laundering and terrorist financing." FATF said it would report on stablecoins in 2020.[210]

Economist and former Greek Minister of Finance Yanis Varoufakis was very impressed with the ideas behind Libra — but not that it was a private company project. He suggested in October that the International Monetary Fund should run a Libra-like coin itself, as an international trading currency. "Brilliant ideas that would be catastrophic in the hands of buccaneering privateers should be pressed into public service."[211]

On 13 October, Randal Quarles, chair of the Financial Stability Board (FSB), wrote a letter to G20 finance ministers and central bank governors discussing the risks of "global stablecoins." The FSB worried that such coins "have the potential to become systemically important, including through the substitution of domestic currencies." The FSB would submit a report in 2020.[212]

Federal Reserve Governor Lael Brainard spoke at the Future of Money in the Digital Age conference on 16 October on "Digital Currencies, Stablecoins, and the Evolving Payments Landscape."[213]

Brainard warned against any entity that wanted to act like a bank without being regulated like a bank. She set out rules for coins like Libra — compliance with Know-Your-Customer regulations, especially across borders; consumer protections like bank accounts have; consumer data protection; and defining just what the "various players in the Libra ecosystem" are doing financially.

Brainard talked up the coming FedNow payment system — to replace the ACH bank transfer system, which could take days to send money, with an instant settlement system, in the manner of the UK's Faster Payments Scheme. This would leave workarounds like Libra more or less superfluous inside the US.

# Bank for International Settlements: "Investigating the impact of global stablecoins"

The twenty-six central banks on the Committee on Payments and Market Infrastructure of the Bank for International Settlements (BIS) invited Libra's founders to Basel, Switzerland, to talk with them on 16 September. The meeting was chaired by Benoît Cœuré of the ECB.[214] Cœuré said after the meeting that stablecoins were "largely untested" at any sort of scale, and that there would be a high bar for regulatory approval.[215]

This meeting fed into the BIS and G7's stablecoin report, started in July and released on 17 October: "Investigating the impact of global stablecoins."[216] The report was closely read by every banker and regulator in the world who was wondering how to respond to Libra, and by the US House before they questioned Mark Zuckerberg.

The report names Libra itself only in the footnotes — but it's all about Libra:

> Some risks are amplified and new risks might arise if adoption is global in nature. Stablecoin initiatives built on an existing — large and/or cross-border — customer base may have the potential to scale rapidly to achieve a global or other substantial footprint. These are referred to as "global stablecoins" (GSCs).

Stablecoin systems are payment systems, and the biggest problem with international payments is not the technology — it's compliance with anti-money-laundering laws. Cryptocurrencies mostly work around this by ignoring it — but Libra couldn't be allowed to do that.

Sound governance is essential. Regulators need confidence that the coin is not being run by slapdash bozos — such as believers in weird Bitcoin economics, which the Committee politely phrases as: "Sound governance may be especially challenging in the case of permissionless DLT systems." (DLT stands for Distributed Ledger Technology, a common euphemism for "blockchain.")

Stablecoins must ensure fair pricing — not only when they're sold directly by the issuer, but in secondary markets. The Committee warned specifically against the sort of shenanigans we see in crypto trading:

> they may have an incentive to disclose untruthful information on their activities, such as the number of

customers and trading volume for advertising and other purposes. Alternatively, stablecoin issuers could intentionally (or unintentionally) mislead their customers on the critical functions they perform, such as the way they manage collateral assets.

A stablecoin must, of course, have robust computer security — they can't be as hackable as the systems in the cryptocurrency world keep turning out to be.

Consumers must be protected — in ways they presently aren't when using cryptocurrencies:

> If there are unauthorised payments from a stablecoin account, there should be clarity on what rights the holder has to claim a refund and clear instructions on how to obtain a refund. Concerns over information and consumer understanding could be exacerbated by misleading marketing and the potential for misselling, as has been observed in the wider cryptoasset market.

Because we're talking about Facebook, the report mentions data protection. Specifically, that if you put anything that may constitute personal data onto a blockchain — a permanent, immutable ledger — you'll run head-first into Europe's General Data Protection Regulation (GDPR), and the "right to be forgotten."

A popular stablecoin will be a systemic risk. A single coin winning in the market could have anti-competitive network effects. The price stabilisation mechanism needs high standards of risk management — and must guard against runs on the coin.

A global stablecoin's reserve might be large enough to affect financial markets — especially if they buy up all the high-quality cash-equivalent assets. Countries with less stable currencies risk sudden Libraisation, the replacement of their local currencies with Libra — particularly "given the inability to hold sovereign-to-sovereign discussions on the public policy implications of such substitution."

The report wasn't entirely negative on global stablecoins. "Recent GSC initiatives have highlighted the shortcomings in cross-border payments and access to transaction accounts, and the importance of improving access to financial services and cross-border retail payments." But the initiatives will have to show that they will actually improve access and payments — not just say that they want to.

# The Libra Association launches

The Libra Association officially formed on 14 October 2019, with the remaining twenty-one members signing on. The founding board was David Marcus, Matthew Davie (Kiva), Patrick Ellis (PayU), Kathryn Haun (Andreessen Horowitz) and Wences Casares (Xapo).[217]

Mark Zuckerberg stressed to Congress on 23 October that the Libra Association was much more than Facebook — and that Facebook might even pull out of the Association if the other members took Libra in a direction Facebook couldn't work with.

But as of October, Facebook was still Libra's only financial backer — and other members said that Libra would fall apart if Facebook pulled out.[218] Association members had yet to put in their $10 million. Members told the BBC that there was no timeline for contributing — though all who were asked said they would likely put their money in: "The feeling is that we needed to form, ratify a budget, and then figure out how to fund that budget, rather than the other way around."[219]

Dante Disparte admitted on 14 October that Libra might not make a 2020 release. "Even though we may be ready with the technology, the regulatory piece is the bit that carries the most uncertainty … Our commitment is that the project will not launch until such time as it has met all the necessary regulatory approvals on both sides of the Atlantic."[220]

# David Marcus on the state of Libra

While Mark Zuckerberg was preparing for the House hearing, David Marcus was meeting Congressional staff, and giving speeches on Libra to a World Bank meeting and to the Group of Thirty (G30), an international group of financiers and academics.

Marcus told the New York Times[221] that politicians had been negative — but he said that regulators had been much more positive in private.

He took credit for bringing the Libra ideas into discussion: "We didn't launch anything. We opened up the idea that maybe it was a good thing to try to do something new to advance the state of access to digital money in general." He told Fortune, "Everyone is now talking about digital currencies around the world — everyone. And if it hadn't come from us, that timeline — to make progress in having the right framework for digital currencies — would have taken much longer."[17]

Marcus didn't regret how Libra was announced, and he disagreed that Facebook should have done more to bring regulators on board ahead of the launch — even as the payment companies who had left the Libra Association earlier in the month specifically cited the lack of engagement with regulators. "Even if we spent ten years outreaching, you'd still hear the same thing."

Marcus claimed the overwhelming negative response was actually *good* news for Libra — "We've advanced the dialogue on the fact that the status quo was not and should not be an option and that we need to move forward with a better system to enable more people to participate in the financial system."

He had just one regret: "If I had to do it all over again, I would probably just focus on what this thing really is, which is a new payment system."

## The end of Libra?

At the Institute of International Finance (IIF) meetings in Washington DC in mid-October, bankers casually spoke in the past tense about Libra — amazed at Facebook's spectacular failures of judgement.[40]

After months of negative reactions, Zuckerberg's House hearing on 23 October was widely seen as the make-or-break moment for Libra — whether a company like Facebook would be allowed to start a financial enterprise of globally systemic scale.

# Chapter 13:
# Mark Zuckerberg before
# the US House

The House Committee on Financial Services was keen to discuss Libra with Mark Zuckerberg, CEO of Facebook — the man who would have the final say on the project. A hearing was announced on 9 October 2019, to be held on 23 October: "An Examination of Facebook and Its Impact on the Financial Services and Housing Sectors." Zuckerberg would be the sole witness testifying, in what turned out to be a six-hour grilling.[222]

After the past few months of the world heaping ordure on Libra, this was Zuckerberg's last chance to make this plan fly with the legislators who could make or break it — and he failed to bring fresh answers.

The Committee had many more questions about Facebook's past and ongoing misbehaviour than they did about Libra itself. But those questions were explicitly about whether Facebook was a fit company to run a scheme like Libra.

Zuckerberg spoke in a clear, relaxed and confident tone — but he was weak on detail. Zuckerberg's glibness contrasted with David Marcus' earnest precision in the July hearing.

Zuckerberg dodged questions about Libra itself by talking about Facebook's Calibra wallet instead, and he punted tricky questions to the "independent" Libra Association — as if Facebook hadn't founded the Association, and wasn't its sole funder. He seemed unclear on many details of the Libra project — including questions that were follow-ups to questions that Marcus had been asked in July.

Both sides of the House were still sceptical of Libra. Bill Huizenga (R, MI-02) commented: "You have accomplished something that nobody, and I mean nobody, thought was possible — Brad Sherman, Chair Waters, many on the other side of the aisle, actually agree with and in fact, use tweets by the President to support their position. I never thought I would see the day, but here we are."

Several House members were quite enthusiastic about Libra. But even they wondered about the details of Libra's anti-money-laundering compliance — particularly given that all the US-based payment processors had suddenly left the Libra Association just weeks before — and why the Association was based in Switzerland if, as Zuckerberg said several times, Libra was an extension of American financial power that was urgently needed to fight China's planned digital coin.

Zuckerberg may have been wondering just what on earth his underlings had dropped him in with this Libra project.

## The hearing opens

Press and staff crowded around the committee room from 7AM. The public gallery filled for the hearing, with queues around the building.[223]

The Chair, Maxine Waters (D, CA-43), launched the proceedings just after 10AM with an excoriation of Facebook. "I've come to the conclusion that it would be beneficial for all if Facebook concentrates on addressing its many existing deficiencies and failures before proceeding any further on the Libra project."[224] [225]

Waters spoke of the many ways that Facebook had "utterly failed." The company had failed on diversity and inclusion. It had been caught in "redlining," when housing advertisements were not shown to users of particular races — which Facebook was being sued for both by the US Department of Housing and Urban Development, and privately by housing charities. Antitrust investigations were active in 47 states and the District of Columbia. The company had been fined $5 billion by the FTC over the Cambridge Analytica scandal. Facebook had enabled the government of Russia to interfere in the 2016 election.

"It's clear to me," said Waters, "and to anyone who hears this list, that perhaps you believe that you're above the law. And given the company size and reach, it should be clear why we have serious concerns about your plans to establish a global digital currency that would challenge the US dollar. In fact, you have opened up a serious discussion about whether Facebook should be broken up."

The Ranking Member, Patrick McHenry (R, NC-10), said that "there's a lot of anger out there, and now it's being directed at the architects of this system. That's why you're here, Mr. Zuckerberg." But he was much more positive about Libra's potential: "If history has taught us anything, it's better to be on the side of American innovation, competition and most importantly the freedom to build a better future for all of us," he said. "American innovation is on trial this day, in this hearing."

Zuckerberg admitted that Facebook had "faced a lot of issues over the past few years, and I'm sure there are a lot of people who wish it were anyone but Facebook who were helping to propose this." He quickly went into the pitch for Libra: "The financial industry is stagnant, and there is no digital, financial architecture to support the innovation that we need. I believe that this problem can be solved and Libra can help." He warned that "China is moving quickly to launch a similar idea in the coming months." He said that Facebook was working on its bias and diversity issues.

## Facebook's past record

This hearing was not just about Libra itself — it was about Facebook's fitness to run a financial institution of systemic scale. Alexandria Ocasio-Cortez's (D, NY-14) grilling of Zuckerberg went viral: "I think you, of all people, can appreciate using a person's past behaviour in order to determine, predict, or make decisions about future behaviour."

Nearly half the representatives present, from both parties, raised serious concerns about Facebook. Many mentioned Facebook's extensive track record of privacy violations — including how Facebook built data profiles on people who weren't even Facebook users — and how they found it hard to believe that Facebook really would keep data from the Calibra wallet sequestered from the Facebook advertising engine, when Facebook had integrated WhatsApp data after promising not to.

Others raised the abuse of Facebook data in biasing elections, including the Cambridge Analytica scandal, and in vote suppression. Ocasio-Cortez questioned Zuckerberg closely on what he knew, and when he knew it. Members were not happy with Facebook refusing to fact-check claims in political advertising. Alma Adams (D, NC-12) and Dean Phillips (D, MN-03) wondered if Libra would become just another tool for bad actors to abuse.

Lacy Clay (D, MO-01) and David Scott (D, GA-13) asked about Facebook's "redlining" housing advertisements. Zuckerberg said that "our policies have always been that discrimination is not allowed" … and how Facebook had entered into a settlement to remove the discrimination that they had been allowing for years.

Madeleine Dean (D, PA-04) asked: "From 2009 until this very year, while under a consent decree to clean up your credibility, your credibility with your customers, to protect their privacy, to protect them from deceptive practices — you failed to do that for 10 years. Am I correct?"

Zuckerberg said that he "wouldn't agree with that characterization." Dean noted that Facebook had been fined $5 billion "in recognition of that failure."

Zuckerberg said to several members that the compliance regimes Facebook had been placed under, owing to its string of repeated violations, were actually *good* news for the company's future good behaviour — because now Facebook was being closely monitored. So letting Libra proceed would work out just fine.

Several representatives really didn't buy this. Jesús "Chuy" García (D, IL-04) put forward the "Keep Big Tech Out Of Finance" discussion draft from July as a bill:[226] "Whenever we have blurred the lines between commerce and banking in this country, we have run into problems. I don't think we can trust you."

Other objections were less substantial. Bill Posey (R, FL-08) chose this hearing to object to Facebook having restricted anti-vaccine activism on the site as misleading health advice. Zuckerberg politely replied that "I don't think it would be possible for anyone to be 100% confident, but my understanding of the scientific consensus is that it is important that people get their vaccines."

## Money laundering and terrorist financing

The House still demanded strong anti-money-laundering (AML) provisions in Libra — to block criminals and terrorists.

Zuckerberg said that Facebook had artificial intelligence technology that would help detect questionable transactions — much as it tried to detect terrorist content on the social network. Denver Riggleman (R, VA-05) asked about algorithmic enforcement of AML rules. Zuckerberg said they were "looking at whether there are elements of the AML or KYC [*Know-Your-Customer*] regulations that can be encoded at the network level."

Zuckerberg said several times that Facebook's Calibra wallet would have solid identity requirements. Carolyn Maloney (D, NY-12) didn't think this was enough: "Will you commit to not supporting any other anonymous wallets for Libra? I consider this a national security issue." But Zuckerberg would only commit for Calibra, and not for Libra itself.

# Libra versus China

Zuckerberg repeatedly pitched Libra as an American weapon against China's plans for a digital coin:

> We need to trade off and think about and weigh any risks of a new system against what I think are surely risks if a Chinese financial system becomes the standard in more countries, because then it would be very difficult, if not impossible, for us to impose our sanctions.

Anthony Gonzalez (R, OH-16) wasn't convinced. "I think you'll be hard pressed to find somebody who's more of a hawk on China in this committee. Like, this isn't Mark Zuckerberg versus Xi Jinping."

Facebook had previously tried and failed to push into China, and Zuckerberg had even started learning Mandarin at one point. "I probably, ten years ago, would have been more optimistic that trying to work in China could have contributed to making a more open society," he said.

Rep. McHenry asked: "You see Alipay and WeChat Pay working. Why not just do a Facebook version of Alipay in order to level this?" Zuckerberg said that the American banking system had a lot of creaky legacy — "part of the infrastructure that they're building on is a lot more modern than some of what we would have to build on here."

Zuckerberg did admit to Andy Barr (R, KY-06) that China had put its programme to start a central bank digital currency into high gear specifically because of Libra — that Facebook had caused the problem they were now selling a solution to:

> As soon as we put out this white paper on Libra, what we saw was, in China, especially, they immediately kicked off this public-private partnership with some of their biggest companies in order to race to try to build a system like this quickly, a digital renminbi.

## Why not just run Libra on dollars?

The US government is understandably fond of the US dollar — as Juan Vargas (D, CA-51) put it, "the dollar is very important to us as a tool of American power, and also a tool of American values. So we would much prefer to put sanctions on a country than send our soldiers there. So when something threatens the dollar, we get very nervous."

Congress wasn't so happy at the idea of Facebook running a non-American basket currency at large enough scale to be a systemic risk. Michael San Nicolas (D, Guam) went into some detail about all the ways a basket reserve could go wrong.

Steve Stivers (R, OH-15) asked: "But why create a private currency? Why not just pick a currency and use that as part of your payment system?" French Hill (R, AR-02) also suggested that Libra should just use dollars. Sylvia Garcia (D, TX-29) said Libra should talk to the Federal Reserve about an official digital dollar.

Zuckerberg answered that Libra was intended to be usable and welcomed globally — though it would be substantially based on the US dollar. He admitted he didn't entirely buy into the basket plan himself — "I, personally, am much more focused on being able to help innovate and build a global payment system than I am in any specific makeup of what a currency or reserve might look like" — and said that they were also discussing a possible system based on individual sovereign currencies.

Zuckerberg was keen to reassure the Committee that the currency basket would mostly be US dollars. "I actually think that a project like this could be important for extending America's financial leadership." He suggested a regulation requiring the basket to be primarily US dollars.

## The Libra Association

Several companies had left the Libra Association earlier in October. None had given reasons officially, but sources at some of the payment processors had told the press that Facebook hadn't given sufficient attention to regulatory compliance.

Ann Wagner (R, MO-02) worried that the payment processors had left because of "concerns whether you're up to the task of meeting our money laundering and regulatory standards." Scott Tipton (R, CO-03) and Ted Budd (R, NC-13) wondered how Libra would do sufficiently strong AML without any of the US payment processors on hand — whether they'd be starting from scratch.

Zuckerberg said that the payment processors had left because Libra was "a risky project, and I think that there's been a lot of scrutiny."

Gregory Meeks (D, NY-05) noted that "you do have a trust factor. I've met with a lot of your investors who are pulling out of Libra."

Al Green (D, TX-09) was concerned that Libra Association member companies were mostly headed by straight white men — "The public needs to know whether this is an organization that is truly diverse or whether it is an organization that is owned and operated by a small group of persons, all of whom have similar characteristics."

Rep. Huizenga and Rep. Gonzalez got Zuckerberg to confirm that if the Libra Association went ahead without US approval, then Facebook would leave the Association.

Lance Gooden (R, TX-05) wanted Libra brought back to the US: "One of the things that was troubling to me was this idea that we've got a great American company like Facebook, and a great American success story like yourself, who's pushing this idea on foreign soil."

Rep. Vargas was pretty sure that Facebook could bring the Libra Association back from Switzerland to the US if it wanted to — "Seems to be falling apart without you guys, frankly. So they don't seem to exist without you. You're the big dog in this fight. Honestly, if you decide to bring it to the United States, it comes to the United States. I mean, you can hide behind that a little bit, but I won't believe it."

Ayanna Pressley (D, MA-07) concurred: "Mr. Zuckerberg, Libra is Facebook, and Facebook is you."

Zuckerberg reiterated that Switzerland was a good place to base Libra as an international organisation — but repeated that "we want to extend American financial leadership across the world."

Rep. Gooden noticed that the Libra Investment Token proposal — where Association members would pay in $10 million each to start the Libra reserve, and get dividends from the interest on the reserve — had been quietly removed from the Libra white papers. Zuckerberg confirmed that the dividend idea had been "modified or abandoned."

## How do you make your money, anyway?

Billion-dollar corporations aren't famous for starting large systems with obvious potential for profit, and handing them to the public for free. Facebook didn't plan to charge fees to use their Calibra wallet, or to make Libra transactions — so what was Facebook getting out of Libra and Calibra?

"The vision here is to make it so that people can send money to each other as easily, and securely, and cheaply as it is to send a text message," said Zuckerberg. "I think that sending money would be a very useful utility to add for people around the world, in addition to the messaging products that we have."

Zuckerberg said that Libra would help encourage direct sales from the Facebook and Instagram Marketplaces. It would reduce friction for businesses on Facebook — and so help sell more ads. Jennifer Wexton (D, VA-10) wondered: "are you going to mine data and use that to monetize the data that you get from people's purchases?" Zuckerberg was quick to state again that Calibra data would not be used in this way.

## Banking the unbanked

Zuckerberg hammered on the "bank the unbanked" message in his written testimony — "more than 14 million people right here in the US" — though it wasn't mentioned much by the members.

Frank Lucas (R, OK-03) asked: "A significant portion of the underbanked simply do not trust banks. I suspect they may not trust captains of industry or members of Congress either, for that matter. How do you persuade those people that you're trustworthy and to use the system?"

Zuckerberg said to Lucas that people kept using Facebook itself, so they clearly trusted the company that much. He told John Rose (R, TN-06) that strong financial regulations meant that consumers could trust that any particular company would follow those rules.

Rep. Meeks wanted more direct action from Facebook, such as working with minority depository institutions (MDIs). "How much of Facebook's money is in MDIs that provide services and help the unbanked and the underbanked? Have you invested in any of the minority development depository institutions in America or any place else in the world?" Zuckerberg didn't know. Meeks guessed the amount was zero, and said that "action speaks much louder than words."

Brad Sherman (D, CA-30) was not impressed. "For the richest man in the world to come here and hide behind the poorest people in the world, and say that's who you're really trying to help, you're trying to help those for whom the dollar is not a good currency. Drug dealers, terrorists, tax evaders."

# The problems with cryptocurrency

Libra was created by Bitcoin fans, who started from Bitcoin ideas and ideals — but none of those ideas would work in a regulated environment, and particularly not if the idea might be a systemic risk at large scale.

Real finance has human oversight and trusted responsibility all through it — and not automated systems that humans can't touch. Unfortunately, Libra's Bitcoin ancestry was still clear in the design of the system.

Bill Foster (D, IL-11) is himself a computer programmer. He had looked at the Libra code, and was particularly concerned that the Libra software allowed anonymous and irreversible transactions:

> It seems to me that if you have the private key, you have control of that Libra balance, period. Full stop. And that makes it pretty hard … it's equivalent to self-custody. And if you allow self-custody, it's pretty hard to stop anonymous trading.

> … From the very start, you have to understand: is there a mechanism to reverse a transaction? All these big Bitcoin billionaires go around with big security details because if someone puts a gun on their head and says, "Give me your Bitcoin," it is not a reversible transaction. And so I don't think people want to live in that kind of situation.

Zuckerberg started answering about the Calibra wallet — but Foster wouldn't be swayed: "No, Libra. Libra. Libra." Zuckerberg kept answering about Calibra, but said that they had not nailed down all the policies on that sort of issue for Libra itself.

A financial system running entirely on smart contract programs on a public blockchain is a big, juicy single target for hackers. Rep. Rose asked who would be liable if the system was hacked. Zuckerberg said it would depend if it was a Facebook service that was hacked — in which case Facebook would be liable — or something deeper in the Libra network; and that this risk would be an appropriate case for regulation.

Zuckerberg told Warren Davidson (R, OH-08) that full decentralisation, in the manner of Bitcoin, was interesting, but it wasn't what Facebook wanted to do: "We're not going to create something that's decentralized that can't hold up the highest standards of protecting against all the risks that we're talking about today, whether it's financial stability or fighting terrorism or crime or fraud."

Rep. Gonzalez, however, was "very positive" about fully decentralised blockchains, and encouraged Zuckerberg to "work on ways to decentralize, so that there is no control whatsoever."

## Who's regulating this?

A basket-based currency that ran at a large enough scale to be a systemic risk would touch every federal financial regulator. Rep. Maloney listed the Federal Reserve, the FDIC (who insure bank deposits), the Office of the Comptroller of the Currency (who regulate banks), the SEC, the CFTC, the Consumer Financial Protection Bureau, FinCEN (money laundering), the Federal Housing Finance Agency, "and many, many more. And to be clear, Libra would affect all of those regulators."

Zuckerberg answered that Libra would be in the ambit of "probably all of them for different things." But he reiterated that Libra and Calibra would get all the appropriate US approvals before launching anywhere in the world.

Emanuel Cleaver (D, MO-05) had written to the Financial Stability Oversight Council (FSOC), and was less sanguine: "I was told that it's unclear whether US and foreign regulators will have the ability to monitor Libra and require any kind of corrective actions. What happens if regulators just throw up their hands and say that, 'we cannot guarantee the soundness of this product'?"

Zuckerberg said that Libra's one-to-one reserve should do most of that job — but that Libra was working with FSOC, and would not launch without their approval as well.

Nydia Velázquez (D, NY-07) asked that Libra wait, not just for regulators, but for explicit approval by Congress — given that the G7 global stablecoin report had just warned of "significant adverse effects, both domestically and internationally." Zuckerberg replied that "Congress exercises significant oversight over the regulators through these committees" — which Velázquez cut off with "So that is a no. Thank you."

## Closing statements

In closing the proceedings, even Rep. McHenry, a fan of Libra — especially in the face of the Chinese threat — was disappointed by the day's testimony: "I'm not sure we've learned anything new here … we still don't have a deeper understanding of how Libra will work."

Delegate San Nicolas, as Vice Chair, repeated members' concerns about "our responsibility as the reserve currency of the world," and Libra basing itself in Switzerland.

Rep. Waters finished the session repeating Facebook's list of past failures and bad behaviour. "I hope that you've heard these concerns and that you will heed our warnings."

San Nicolas struck the gavel to adjourn the hearing just after 4PM. Zuckerberg stood, chatted and shook hands with several members, spoke with Waters and McHenry for a few minutes each, then left the room through the back door.

## How did Zuckerberg do?

This hearing did not advance Libra at all — it mainly focused attention on Facebook's past bad behaviour.

Zuckerberg was on defense. He understood that this hearing was going to be about Facebook, and that his job was to take the heat. He used Libra to deflect from Facebook's other sins — and Libra became a sideshow at its own hearing.

But Zuckerberg was vaguest on the Libra-specific questions. The only mitigation of the original Libra plan that Zuckerberg offered was to use various local currencies, rather than a basket-based Libra currency.

The members were unimpressed by Zuckerberg's attempts to dodge behind the Libra Association, and how he answered questions about Libra by talking about Facebook's Calibra. They didn't buy China as an excuse either.

Zuckerberg realised he wasn't going to charm anyone here with Libra, and noticeably brightened up when talking about a "big initiative around news and journalism" instead, which was launched a few days later as Facebook News.

Zuckerberg maintained face — but he didn't convince the House to let Libra go ahead.

# Chapter 14:
# November 2019: The comedown

One marker of the progress made by blockchain bros in 2019 is that "Facebook: the most trusted name in cryptocurrency" remains both a joke and a statement of fact.

— Financial Times FT Alphaville[227]

After Mark Zuckerberg's appearance before the House, Facebook was generally considered to have blown it with Libra — there was no way the US would let anything that was within a mile of Facebook's original plan go ahead.

But the idea was still in the air, and banks and regulators were still considering what to do about future proposals of this sort. And, of course, Facebook's Calibra unit and the fresh new Libra Association were still trying to work out what they could make happen.

Zuckerberg himself has not spoken or written of Libra in public since the October 2019 House hearing — except passing mentions during Facebook earnings calls.

## Facebook's bottom line

Facebook's reputation had taken a beating, and their corporate sins had been brought up afresh in Zuckerberg's House hearing — but Facebook was still a money machine.

In the third quarter of 2019, Facebook's earnings per share were $2.12, up 20% compared to the third quarter of 2018. Total revenues were $17.7 billion — up 29% year-on-year.

Mark Zuckerberg's third quarter of 2019 earnings call,[228] on 30 October, mentioned Libra only in passing — it was one of "multiple exciting initiatives around commerce and payments that are moving forward," and part of "our work with something like Libra that is trying to build some new technological infrastructure for financial services."

Facebook's Chief Financial Officer, Dave Wehner, said there was "no update right now on the timetable on the 2020 launch" and that Libra was "in a holding pattern as far as getting to a point where we've got regulatory approval."

# Calibra stays the course

Calibra staff remained enthusiastic — and talked up Libra's future as the single system to rule them all.

In late October, Christian Catalini explicitly positioned Libra as the new central system for finance: "The idea is to create a platform that is fully interoperable, where different financial institutions can all use the same infrastructure and be compatible. This addresses the fragmented nature of payments systems today."[99]

Catalini dismissed the possibility of Libra taking over small economies, saying that "Libra at present is optimised as a medium of exchange to enable cheap and fast payments, which is very different to a currency role" — which didn't in any way answer how such Libraisation of an economy wouldn't then happen just as everyone else could see it happening. And most people would think that being "a medium of exchange to enable cheap and fast payments" was a currency role.

Kevin Weil spoke at San Francisco Blockchain Week on 31 October[229] and Web Summit on 5 November.[230] He posited Libra as an Internet or text-message network of payments — you had all these payment providers that didn't talk to each other, but if they were all backed by Libra then they could interoperate: "Can we do for money what the internet did for communication?" This harked back to Peter Thiel's 1999 pitch for PayPal as "the Microsoft of payments, the financial operating system of the world" as we noted earlier.

# The Libra Association: new members

The Libra Association finalised its Articles of Association in November 2019,[231] updated from the original July version.[232] The mission statement was changed from "empowering billions of people through a new global currency" to the rather less snappy "create a lower-cost, more accessible payment tool built on the Libra blockchain that will facilitate a more connected global payment system, providing financial or other services to those most in need of such services."

In January 2020, the Association appointed a Technical Steering Committee — to manage the technical development of this project that didn't have any fixed business specification as yet, and that regulators might never allow to launch.[233]

Membership was now free — members could lend money to the Association, but would not be advantaged in governance.

Vodafone quit the Association in January 2020. Vodafone said that if they were going to put actual money and engineering effort into financial inclusion, their own M-Pesa seemed like a better prospect.[234] It did, after all, have a track record of success.

New 2020 members included Shopify, an e-commerce platform;[235] Tagomi, a cryptocurrency prime brokerage;[236] Heifer International, who provide financial and technological support to small farmers in developing countries;[237] Checkout.com, a UK payments processor;[238] crypto hedge fund Paradigm; private equity firm Slow Ventures;[239] Blockchain Capital, a crypto venture capital firm;[240] and Singapore government-owned sovereign wealth fund Temasek Holdings.

Temasek is the smaller of the two funds (the larger being GIC Private Limited) that keeps Singapore economically healthy and the Singapore dollar on an even keel — with $210 billion of assets under management, it was a hefty player to see joining Libra. This may have been in response to Libra's previous plans to add the Singapore dollar to the Libra basket — which could have badly destabilised the currency. It seems likely that Temasek joined so they'd be on the inside, and not the outside.

## Regulators stay wary

The International Organization of Securities Commissions (IOSCO) discussed "global stablecoins" as part of its October 2019 board meeting, and issued a statement: "So-called 'stablecoins' can include features that are typical of regulated securities. This means IOSCO Principles and Standards may apply to stablecoins depending on how they are structured".[241]

In Congress, Sylvia Garcia (D, TX-29) and Lance Gooden (R, TX-05) introduced the Managed Stablecoins are Securities Act of 2019 — they were pretty sure that things like Libra were already securities, but wanted to nail it down.[242] If you ask for regulatory clarity …

On 5 December 2019, the European Union's Council and Commission bluntly stated that they would block "global stablecoins" until regulators' and central bankers' many concerns were fully addressed. "Tackling the challenges raised by 'global stablecoins' requires a coordinated global response … the Council and the Commission state that no global 'stablecoin' arrangement should begin operation in the European Union until the legal, regulatory and oversight challenges and risks have been adequately identified and addressed."[243]

SRF News spoke to outgoing Swiss President Ueli Maurer on 27 December 2019:[244]

> Q. Libra as it's currently presented — has it any chance at all?
>
> A. I don't think so, because having a basket of currencies backing this currency is not going to be accepted by the national banks. The project in this form has actually failed.

# Consumers: still not interested

In February 2020, the Official Monetary and Financial Institutions Forum (OMFIF) ran a poll on digital payments across 13 countries. The people they surveyed were not happy with the idea of tech companies issuing currencies — but were much happier with the idea of central banks issuing currencies. In fact, central banks were the most trusted financial institutions.[245]

# Facebook Pay: doing 100% of the useful bit of Libra

> If Libra is the Thanksgiving turkey you tried deep frying but caught on fire, Facebook Pay is the backup rotisserie chicken.
>
> — Alex Hickey, Morning Brew[246]

On 12 November 2019, Facebook announced Facebook Pay — a way to send money between Facebook users or businesses. Facebook Pay was available to US users of Facebook and Messenger, with plans to add the service to Instagram and WhatsApp, and to release it in other countries.[247]

Facebook Pay was a rebranded version of Messenger Pay (or Messenger Payments — its branding was never very clear), which originally launched on 17 March 2015, when David Marcus was still running Messenger.

Messenger Pay was for person-to-person payments — it was a direct competitor to PayPal's Venmo. Over its first two years in the US, most transactions were less than $50.

To use Messenger Pay, you connected your existing Visa or Mastercard debit card as a back end. To send someone money, you opened a message to that person, tapped the "$" icon, entered an amount and tapped "pay." You could receive money by connecting your debit card for the money to be sent to.[248]

Messenger Pay didn't charge a transaction fee — what Facebook got out of this was keeping you on the platform, and showing you ads. And, of course, that juicy personal financial data.[249]

The catch was that Messenger Pay ran atop the existing US banking system — transactions between banks could take days.

The service opened in the UK and France in November 2017. Facebook's announcement post called Messenger Pay "one of the most requested features in Messenger." Unfortunately, this didn't translate into demand — the UK and French versions of Messenger Pay were shut down on 15 June 2019, apparently from a lack of users.[250]

But even in the US, Messenger Pay was never popular — and the service remained barely known, as either Messenger Pay or Facebook Pay.

You may be on Facebook lots — but would you trust Facebook with your money? For most people, the answer was "no."

So what did Facebook Pay mean for Libra? Facebook's only comment was their press release statement:

> Facebook Pay is built on existing financial infrastructure and partnerships, and is separate from the Calibra wallet which will run on the Libra network.

The money transmitters did the hard bits of Know-Your-Customer, and Facebook just brought the users along and collected the data — the things it was good at.

Facebook Pay did 100% of the useful part of the Libra idea — and in a way that played to Facebook's strengths, and not its weaknesses.

Facebook probably didn't spend two years building blockchain-based castles in the air, going through three Congressional hearings, and invoking kill-it-with-fire loathing from financial regulators around the world, just to make a consolidated payments app look less threatening by comparison. But that would certainly be an added bonus.

# Mark Zuckerberg's vision for 2030

On 9 January 2020, Mark Zuckerberg posted his personal challenge for the year to his Facebook. But this time, he made it a personal challenge for the decade — "what I hope the world and my life will look in 2030."[251]

Zuckerberg spun a vision of small, private social networks, virtual and augmented reality, generational change, how to govern a digital community, and "decentralized opportunity" — and his example was a world where you could "send money home to another country instantly and at low cost through WhatsApp."

Not mentioned at any point: the word "Libra."

# Chapter 15:
# Central bank digital currencies

He had his cash money, but you couldn't pay for food with that. It wasn't actually illegal to have the stuff, it was just that nobody ever did anything legitimate with it.

— William Gibson, *Count Zero*

Central banks issue physical cash — but what if they could print official legal tender digitally? The real world result from Libra may turn out to be "central bank digital currency," or "CBDC."

A central bank's job is to keep its economy on an even keel. Central bank researchers look at a new idea and think: "what would happen if this weird thing got popular?" The structure of money can change surprisingly fast.

So the researchers routinely come up with wild plans to rebuild the financial system, but upside-down and inside-out — just in case they suddenly need them.

Bankers noticed Bitcoin and other cryptocurrencies early. When people talk about a new form of "money," and there are news headlines about the price of Bitcoin, central bank research papers will follow.

Then Libra threatened to put the idea of a blockchain-like currency into practice, at massive scale — but badly. Central bank researchers quickly dusted off their old papers, with an eye to heading off disaster. And if there was anything to the Libra idea, maybe it could be implemented with an eye to caution.

Central banks have issued electronic money before — but current discussion of "CBDC" involves a lot of misapplied blockchain hype. End users don't need to worry too much about this particular back-end plumbing.

## What is a central bank digital currency?

E-money (electronic money) is money for consumers that's transmitted electronically outside the banking system itself. PayPal is a well known example. A central bank digital currency is e-money issued directly by the central bank — it's regulated differently, but the end user shouldn't see much difference.

Central banks had been thinking about what central-bank-issued e-money might mean since the 1990s[252] — but the current round of CBDC discussion was largely inspired by Bitcoin and blockchains.

CBDC on a blockchain was first suggested in 2013 by economics blogger J. P. Koning as "Fedcoin."[253] Koning proposed that the US Federal Reserve run a widely-distributed blockchain-based database, and create and destroy dollar tokens on the chain as needed. This could also be a consumer payment system, running on your phone.[254] [255]

Central banks wrote papers on what a popular retail CBDC might mean, and what the economic risks might be.

For a long time, all of this was just an academic exercise — with a fair bit of blockchain hype. But as CBDC proposals get closer to reality, they tend to have less and less to do with blockchains.

Some proposals are for wholesale CBDC — between the central banks and the commercial banks — though it's not yet clear what this gets anyone over the banks just sending numbers between known and trusted computers, as we've done for decades. Banks have experimented with blockchains, but the results are, at best, slightly worse, slower and less sophisticated versions of existing systems. Wholesale CBDC is mostly blockchain hype, and mainly of interest to the sort of crypto news site that thinks CBDCs are good news for Bitcoin.

# Responding to Libra with CBDC

Libra frightened the central banks — a popular private currency run by people who didn't seem to know what they were doing could be disastrous.

Central banks started looking into CBDC with more urgency. There might be a gap in the market, mainly for low-cost international settlement — and Facebook said Libra could fill that need. But Libra would run at a large enough scale to risk financial stability.

So central banks would need to do a coin themselves — one that was responsible to the public, rather than to a private company or consortium. The People's Bank of China finally kicked its CBDC programme into high gear in direct response to Libra. (Though they were also reacting to US dollar hegemony and the size of the local payment providers.)

It wasn't clear that Libra could in fact do what it claimed — nor was it clear that a central bank version would do the job either.

# Why do a CBDC?

If you live in Europe or China, you probably have good electronic payment systems — within your country, at least. So you know that good payment systems are possible without adding a blockchain. Other countries are different — because local conditions are important.

* The US is an advanced economy — but the payment system is old, creaky and complicated, and payment companies have to register federally and in fifty states.

* Many countries still run on physical cash, cheques and so on. But better payment systems speed up the flow of money, and get the economy moving faster.

* Even in Europe, the systems inside a country will be fast — but payments between countries may still be slow or expensive.

* Sweden has the opposite problem. Cash is used less and less — but some sort of cash is considered to be socially necessary, and the Riksbank, Sweden's central bank, worries about how to manage an economy with almost no central bank cash in it.

Maybe CBDCs will fix all of these problems! Somehow. Libra also promised to fix all of these problems — somehow.

## Watching every move you make

Physical cash doesn't have Know Your Customer (KYC) — your transactions are private (unless they're large). But one thing that the anti-money-laundering (AML) agencies have required of digital cash so far is KYC. So they would want a CBDC to have KYC.

The idea of all transactions being on a blockchain also appeals to the anti-money-laundering agencies — imagine having a complete ledger of your entire economy. No criminal transaction could escape.

Bureaucrats also keep being seduced by the prospect of a full Eye of Sauron panopticon of every transaction in the economy. This appeals to those who think their problem is not having enough knowledge to exert control as finely as they'd like to.

This is otherwise known as the Big Data Fallacy — where you think that just getting enough data will surely solve all your problems. It's a fallacy because your problems are usually political — you know perfectly well what you need to do, and you're hoping the big data will help convince others to let you do it.

Nevertheless, bureaucrats and anti-money-laundering agencies find the prospect of a CBDC with a full record of everything hard to resist.

Libra would record *less* data centrally — a lot of transactions would happen internally to Facebook's Calibra/Novi, and not even make it outside of that company to be recorded on the main blockchain.

# Can CBDCs give us better payment systems?

A common fallacy of CBDC proposals is thinking that changing the back-end is all you need to make a better payment system.

CBDC proposals tend to have a disconcerting lack of detail about what magic a CBDC will bring that the commercial banks couldn't do better — and that commercial banks haven't done better in other countries. A lot of CBDC plans have been vague, and don't offer much that's new.

Facebook claims Libra can give us better payment and settlement systems. Facebook's method appears to be to ignore regulations. Central banks can't do that.

Agustín Carstens of BIS acknowledged in June 2019: "There needs to be evidence for demand for central bank digital currencies and it is not clear that the demand is there yet. Perhaps people can do what they want by using electronic wallets provided by banks or fintech companies. It depends on the development of payment systems."[256]

Retail CBDCs are only useful if they let you do something that wouldn't be possible without them. But current payment systems are pretty good, and mostly just need to be put into place in infrastructure-poor economies.

The more solid CBDC plans aim to get the commercial banks to build better inter-bank payment systems. A central bank may even build a CBDC system to kickstart better retail payment systems.

# Real-world retail CBDCs

Central banks have issued electronic money for broad public use twice before: Avant in Finland, and Sistema de Dinero Electrónico in

Ecuador. Both failed — Avant wasn't as convenient as debit cards, and Ecuador's central bank just wasn't trusted by the populace.

Uruguay ran a very limited CBDC proof-of-concept over 2017 and 2018, which involved a small number of ordinary end users.

China's DC/EP proposal — which isn't live yet — will be accepted by end users to the degree it works as well as Tenpay/WeChat Pay or Alipay.

New systems in pilot tests with real end users include the Bahamas Sand Dollar and the Eastern Caribbean DCash.

These are very different from each other, and show the many success and failure modes of projects labeled "CBDC."

## Finland: Avant (1993)

The very first CBDC was Avant-Kortti ("Avant Card"), which was launched by the Bank of Finland in 1993.[257]

Avant was a stored value smart card — you bought a card with money on it that you could then spend. From 1994, you could top up an Avant card with more money. The encrypted smart card was far more secure than the magnetic stripe debit and credit cards of the time. So this was e-money, but backed by the central bank.

Cards were anonymous and individual transactions weren't tracked, so money on Avant would work like cash. The card was labeled an "electronic purse" — the Bank of Finland hoped Avant would replace small change. Though users couldn't exchange Avant money between themselves directly — this was possible in the design, but that function was not enabled.

Avant fit most modern definitions of CBDC — it was in the national currency, it was entirely electronic, the money was a claim against the central bank, it was a widely accepted payment instrument, and it didn't need to be continuously online to a central authority. The main difference to modern schemes was that Avant didn't start from blockchain ideas.

The money in Avant was not legal tender — despite being issued by the central bank — so that merchants would not be legally required to accept it in payment of debts, which would have required them to buy expensive terminals.

In 1995, the Bank of Finland sold Avant's operator, Toimiraha, to a consortium of commercial banks. This made no difference to the users — nothing changed about the system.

Avant was one of the first examples of regulated e-money, and informed the European Union's E-money Directive of 2000.

Avant was moderately popular — at its peak there were 900,000 cards in active use, in a country of five million people.

The biggest problem was that users were unhappy at being charged a fee for loading and unloading money, especially as ATM withdrawals were free by this time. Users hated fees more than they liked anonymity. Avant was discontinued at the end of March 2006.

# Ecuador: Sistema de Dinero Electrónico (2014)

The Sistema de Dinero Electrónico (SDE; "electronic money system"), run by the Banco Central del Ecuador (BCE), was a bit odd. For one thing, the currency was the US dollar. For another, the BCE didn't quite have the powers you'd expect of something called a "central bank."

SDE wasn't quite a CBDC — in practical terms, it was really a failed payment system.

Ecuador went through a hyperinflation in the late 1990s. The national currency, the sucre, went down in value rapidly, and the economy was already substantially running on cash in US dollars — so the government chose dollarisation, and formally declared the US dollar the national currency of Ecuador in January 2000.

This left the central bank unable to issue its national currency, act as the lender of last resort, or manage monetary policy in any meaningful way. So the BCE's focus shifted to guidelines and policy. It was also the regulator for payments.

In 2014, Ecuador's Congress approved a fully-backed electronic dollar — so this was technically the first CBDC US dollar, sort of! The system was launched as SDE.

Each dollar in SDE was backed by a dollar stored at the central bank. BCE was the only legal issuer of e-money — cryptocurrency was also disallowed — and the phone company, CNT, was the only legal distribution channel.

You could sign up with an Ecuadorian identity card and a mobile phone. This gave you an account at the BCE. You could go to an authorised outlet and deposit cash into the account.

The stated reason for SDE was to improve access to the banking system for poorer residents, and reduce the reliance of the economy on physical cash, to get the economy moving.

Users could exchange dollars on SDE between themselves, just like cash. The poor ran on a cash economy, a lot of which was an informal economy, and the central bank hoped that SDE would bring them into the financial system.

Both local commentators and foreign debtors worried that Ecuador would create unbacked dollars in SDE to fund government spending and pay off the country's debts — particularly given that the government had defaulted on bond issues just a few years before.[258] But Ecuador denied any such plans, and didn't end up doing anything along these lines with the dollars in SDE.[259]

SDE had a limited launch in late 2014 and a full public launch in 2015. The BCE expected 500,000 users by the end of 2015.

SDE failed to take off — the system only had 5,000 users by the end of 2015. By the end of 2017, SDE had moved $62 million via 5.1 million transactions in its entire existence[260] — with only $11 million on deposit, as compared to the $24.5 *billion* in cash in the Ecuadorian economy. There were 402,515 e-money accounts — but less than 30% of these were ever used, at all.[261]

Ecuadorians with money trusted private banks more than they trusted the central bank — because they remembered the ways the government had abused its financial powers in recent years.[262]

Nor was SDE taken up by the unbanked or underbanked.[263] Even in the rural areas — "Aquí pagamos con la palabra y el dinero contante y sonante" ("here, we pay with our word, and hard cash") — people trusted their local co-op bank, but they didn't trust the central bank.

The central bank just wasn't good at serving retail customers, either — even if it had had the full trust of the users.

The government eventually acknowledged SDE wasn't going to do the job. The commercial and cooperative banks put together a new mobile payment system, Bimo, with BCE as the regulator. SDE was shut down in March 2018, and accounts could be migrated to Bimo.[264]

The main lesson of SDE is: don't try to back your system with a bank that your users don't trust with their money.

## Uruguay: e-Peso (2017)

Banco Central del Uruguay (BCU) issued an e-Peso in a public pilot programme that ran from November 2017 to April 2018. The pilot was part of an official push for financial inclusion.[265]

BCU issued 20 million e-pesos. Commercial banks were not involved in the pilot — though once it started, some banks approached BCU asking if they could join in. Digital wallets were operated centrally by Antel, the national phone company.

The 10,000 end users could hold a maximum of 30,000 e-pesos in their wallet, and registered participating businesses could hold 200,000 per wallet. Users could transfer money to each other — if they had phone coverage. Transaction data was encrypted, but could be decrypted if legally required.

To encourage participation, the first thousand users got a 500 e-peso credit, and there were monthly lotteries for the most active users and businesses.

The pilot finished in April 2018. The e-pesos were cashed out and destroyed.

BCU considered the pilot a success — the system basically worked on a small scale, and commercial banks wanting to join suggested that such a system could be popular. BCU is still considering whether to do a full-scale public e-Peso — the technical bit works, and now they're going through the economic risk assessments.

## Bahamas: Sand Dollar (2020)

The Central Bank of the Bahamas (CBB) wanted to encourage an electronic payment system that reached the outer islands of the Bahamas — the cash infrastructure was shrinking as commercial banks closed branches, but phone coverage was surprisingly good, if patchy.

Electronic payment systems for retail were usually built by commercial banks. But in this case, the central bank figured it needed to push things forward.[266]

The CBB started with a list of what they needed in an electronic payment system, and worked out the system from there — something to handle spotty network coverage and lots of poor prospective users, but almost all of whom had phones.

Most users connected via their bank account — the CBB left retail to the retail banks. Users who didn't have bank accounts could get a Sand Dollar wallet with their name, address, phone number and a photo, which was enough to open a very limited account at a retail money changer.

The Sand Dollar wallet app on your phone could transmit small amounts of money when you were offline.

The Sand Dollar pilot in 2020 was small — just $48,000 in circulation in the system[267] — but it went well, and the system was set to go live across the Bahamas in late 2020.

## Eastern Caribbean: DCash (2020)

DCash, from the Eastern Caribbean Central Bank (ECCB), started its pilot programme in late 2020 — with real consumers and merchants using it for real transactions.[268]

DCash had similar local conditions to the Bahamas Sand Dollar initiative. However, the system had no offline capability at the pilot stage — you had to be online.

Most DCash end users worked through their banks, with limited accounts available for unbanked users.

DCash had a blockchain in the system, though it was just an instance of IBM's Hyperledger running as a back-end data store, and not doing anything you couldn't do just as well without a blockchain.

## China: DC/EP (in testing)

Digital Cash/Electronic Payments, or DC/EP, is a payment system project by the People's Bank of China (PBOC), carrying central-bank-backed digital renminbi (yuan).

PBOC started looking into blockchains in 2014, and officially established the Digital Currency Research Institute in 2017, which had looked into CBDCs. In the wake of Facebook's June 2019 announcement of Libra, Wang Xin of the PBOC said on 8 July 2019 that they were stepping up their CBDC project,[141] to turn it into something that would stand up to public use at scale.

DC/EP has the following design goals:

- **Two-tier design.** PBOC issues the money, the commercial banks distribute it — the central bank is not going to try to do retail itself.

- **Interoperability.** You can't send payments between the big private money transmitters, Tenpay/WeChat Pay and Alipay — but all DC/EP providers will be interoperable.

- **Financial inclusion.** PBOC gave no specific plan to achieve financial inclusion, though there were aspirations to reach remote and rural populations.

- **Traceability of all transactions.** WeChat Pay and Alipay don't give the central bank full logs of every transaction.

Some in the PBOC are seduced by the prospect of a full record of the entire Chinese economy.

- **"Controllable" anonymity.** You will be anonymous to the retailer — but the central bank still gets a full feed of who's doing what.
- **Working offline.** You should be able to exchange money without being online 24/7. Transactions will be sent in when you're back online.

PBOC found that even relatively fast permissioned blockchains were too slow in internal testing. DC/EP would have to be able to handle at least 300,000 transactions per second across the country at peak times to do what cash does. So DC/EP won't be a blockchain. (The system will apparently contain some sort of blockchain descendant.) Mu Changchun, leader of the DC/EP initiative, co-authored a paper that recommended not to use blockchains to transform traditional payment systems.[269]

PBOC would like DC/EP to replace physical cash to some degree — "M0," the physical cash in the economy. The money in DC/EP will be legal tender, just as paper notes are.[270]

The financial press, as well as the crypto press, leapt upon every new morsel of information about DC/EP — the PBOC had to keep stating that there was no release date as yet. The trickiest part was not the technology — it was regulatory issues, particularly around anti-money-laundering and tax evasion.[271]

The press covered what looked very like public pilot programmes in several areas from late 2019 on — even as the PBOC insisted on calling these only "internal and closed pilot tests." PBOC Governor Yi Gang also mentioned testing in "some scenarios of the coming Winter Olympics" in 2022. He stressed again that there was no release date as yet.[272]

Pilot tests continue through late 2020, at increasing scale.

# Why would I want a CBDC?

Consumers want systems that make their lives easier. Convenience is king. Nobody is going to choose a new payment system that's less convenient.

The users won't care who issues the dollars, pounds or euros, if they can assume basic legal protections — they'll only care how easily they can get, move and spend them.

If you're in a country with good electronic payment systems, a retail CBDC probably won't do anything new for you. The Reserve Bank of Australia decided against a CBDC in 2020, because, even with the decline in cash use in the COVID-19 crisis, existing systems were still working fine, and there was still good access to physical cash.[273]

If you're a banker, of course, it matters a lot who the money is a liability against. But for anyone else, knowing that a payment system is a "CBDC" tells you nothing else about that system. If someone wants you to get excited because something is a CBDC, look closely at what the system does and doesn't do.

If you're Facebook, you might want to run blockchain CBDC tokens over your network instead of Libra tokens — in Libra 2.0.

# Epilogue:
# Libra 2.0: not dead yet

> There is no innovation whatsoever. They have literally
> invented nothing. Libra is possibly the least innovative
> project to ever come out of Silicon Valley.
>
> — Aleksi Grym[274]

Facebook's 2019 plan for a basket-based cryptocurrency had been resoundingly rejected. Governments around the world had finally said "no" to a piece of Silicon Valley "creative destruction."

But it wasn't in Facebook's nature to give up on the quest for personal data. On 16 April 2020, the Libra Association released the Libra White Paper, version 2.0 — in the hope of making financial regulators a bit less unhappy with them.

The Libra network would run individual tokens representing national currencies, starting with dollars, pounds and euros.

The idea of taking Libra fully permissionless was officially abandoned. Only permitted entities would be able to add transactions to the Libra blockchain — not individuals. And anti-money-laundering (AML) functionality would be built into the Libra blockchain itself.

Facebook was forced to transform its great plan into PayPal-but-it's-Facebook — or Libra wouldn't be allowed to exist. Though the back-end system would still run on a blockchain — for no functional reason, but they could say it was on a blockchain.

## Floating the national currency plan

David Marcus and Mark Zuckerberg both floated the idea of Libra using national currency coins in October 2019 — Zuckerberg speaking to Congress, and Marcus to a banking seminar in the US.[275]

Several sources told the Financial Times in February 2020 that the Association had been developing a plan for a "Libra 2.0," to address US regulators' concerns.[276]

In early March, stories about the Libra national currency token scheme ran in Bloomberg[277] and The Information.[278] The basket-based Libra token would run alongside the national tokens, somehow.

On 16 April 2020, the Libra Association proudly announced that it had formally initiated with FINMA, the Swiss regulator, the process of becoming licensed as a payment system.[279]

FINMA did its own press release as well, emphasising that it wasn't just going to let Libra through without checking with everyone else — "FINMA has been in close contact with the Swiss National Bank and more than 20 other supervisory authorities and central banks from around the world since the start of its dealings with the Libra project ... FINMA has always emphasised that the planned international scope of the project requires an internationally coordinated approach."[280]

# The Libra White Paper v2.0

The press release came with a heavily revised version of the Libra white paper. The new white paper still had the wild aspirations to crypto-fueled unregulated finance — but there were also extensive concessions to regulators, which meant that none of that stuff could be allowed to happen any more.[281]

## National currency tokens and the native Libra

The national currency tokens would be electronic coins on the Libra network. At that point, the Libra Association would just be an e-money provider.

The Libra Association also wanted to run CBDCs on the system as they became available. This would save messing about with managing a reserve, if the tokens themselves were the money.

What about Libra the token? The Association still wanted to do their custom currency. The plan was to run the Libra currency as a smart contract program that would balance fixed proportions of national currency tokens in the background, in some manner.

The composition of the native Libra currency was not yet decided. The white paper suggested handing control of the basket to "a group of regulators and central banks or an international organization" under the guidance of FINMA — rather than doing it themselves.

## The Libra reserve(s)

The new white paper mentioned "key concerns" with Facebook's original Libra reserve plan — that is, every financial regulator in the world coughing up their own skulls in horror — and in particular, the

October 2019 paper from the G7 Working Group on Stablecoins, where "stablecoin" was the standard central bank euphemism for "Libra."

The national currency tokens would each be backed by a reserve denominated in that currency. Each reserve would include a capital buffer, to deal with investment losses, negative yields or liquidity problems. Facebook wanted so very much to run a private currency that they would put their own money into this.

If economic conditions meant Libra dealers stopped redeeming tokens from the Libra network for actual money, the Association — that is, Facebook — would step in to redeem tokens directly.

The white paper listed various other emergency scenarios. These all looked rather like stress test provisions for banks.

The Association planned to deal with the threat of Libraisation — a country's economy being taken over by Libras — after it happened, maybe:

> In particular, if adoption in a region without a single-currency stablecoin on the network generates concerns about currency substitution, then the Association could work with the relevant central bank and regulators to make a stablecoin available on the Libra network.

## Permissioned compliance

If you're doing e-money, Know-Your-Customer on the individual customers isn't enough — anti-money-laundering rules require you to watch the movements of the e-money itself.

The new white paper acknowledged that the Libra system would need a full regulatory compliance framework, or it wouldn't be allowed to exist. The Association couldn't just leave compliance to the Libra dealer network, as they'd been hoping to. The Libra system would need to be fully conformant with financial compliance, risk management and anti-money-laundering rules, at the network level.

The Libra network would only be open to designated Libra dealers and regulated cryptocurrency exchanges — "Virtual Asset Service Providers," as defined by the Financial Action Task Force, in FATF-compliant jurisdictions.

The Association still hoped to make the network open to anyone to use — because their new solution to "banking the unbanked" was for individual end users to run Libra software themselves ("Unhosted Wallets"), and access a future public Libra blockchain directly:

Unhosted Wallets enable financial inclusion, broad competition, and responsible innovation and thus facilitate the creation of services for the unbanked and underbanked. Since their activities may pose a greater risk, they will be subject to balance and transaction limits.

But there was no chance of regulators letting anything like this happen — direct personal access to the blockchain was too obviously a channel to launder money. You'd deal with the Libra network through a provider with full Know-Your-Customer checks and compliance mechanisms in place, or you wouldn't deal with it at all.

## Making money 2.0

Facebook removed the Libra Investment Token scheme from the Libra white papers in July 2019, and replaced it with a scheme of unspecified Libra coin "incentives." The wording in the White Paper 2.0 was "incentive programs to propel the adoption of the Libra payment system".

The 2.0 white paper does not mention user data protection, nor privacy.

# Regulators respond

In US Congress, Rep. Sylvia Garcia wasn't mollified: "Facebook and the Libra Association have issued a second white paper that retains a Libra coin backed by a basket of assets. As such, this does not address the concerns I raised when Mr Zuckerberg testified before the Financial Services Committee."[282]

Experts still considered Facebook the biggest issue with any Libra plan. "The political barriers to Libra getting off the ground are still there," said Ben Koltun of Beacon Policy Advisors to the Financial Times.[283]

Central banks and financial regulators still kept the closest possible eye on Libra-like ideas — because even if it was payments-focused and based on national currencies, a popular Libra-like coin could still be a systemic risk.

The Financial Action Task Force reported to the G20 finance ministers on "so-called stablecoins" in July 2020.[284] Andrew Bailey, then of the Bank of England, spoke in September 2020 on how to regulate "global stablecoins."[285] The European Union announced a new college of supervisors in September 2020 to regulate "significant e-money tokens" — that is, Libra-like coins.[286]

The Financial Stability Board ran its promised consultation on "global stablecoins" in April 2020,[287] delivering a final report on 13 October 2020: "Regulation, Supervision and Oversight of 'Global Stablecoin' Arrangements."[288] This was another report that didn't mention Libra by name, but was entirely about Libra. The section on cross-border payments referenced requirements that were set out in another report the FSB released on the same day, "Enhancing Cross-border Payments: Stage 3 roadmap," which stretched to 2023 at the earliest — possibly holding up international payments being run over Libra until then.[289]

# WhatsApp Pay Brazil: no lessons learned

Facebook Pay was the back end for Facebook's attempt to enter the Brazilian payments market with WhatsApp Pay in June 2020.

Facebook took the same approach with Brazilian regulators that they'd taken with Libra — they gave them only the vaguest details, then tried to launch at sufficiently large scale that it would be politically difficult to shut them down once they were up and running.

Banco Central do Brasil (BCB) president Roberto Campos Neto said: "Prior to the launch, there was a meeting in which WhatsApp kind of explained its plan, but the central bank was taken by surprise with the launch on June 15."[290]

Facebook tried to launch the system in Brazil through a loophole: a company could start a payment service without a license until it reached 500 million reals in volume, or 25 million transactions, over a 12-month period. But this was meant to encourage small businesses into the market — it wasn't meant for an existing network with 120 million users in the country.

The loophole Facebook had used was closed on 23 June, and BCB promptly told Mastercard and Visa to cut off payments through WhatsApp.[291] CADE, the Brazilian competition regulator, suspended WhatsApp's partnership with local payment provider Cielo for a week.

Local commenters suggested that Facebook was trying to monopolise quick payments in Brazil, before the local real-time retail settlement system PIX came online in November 2020 — that is, a foreign corporate proprietary system to push out a local open standard.

WhatsApp Pay Brazil was finally allowed to proceed as a strictly limited pilot in July. Campos Neto was still concerned about Facebook's record on data protection.[292]

## Calibra becomes Novi at Facebook Financial

Facebook renamed Calibra in May 2020 as Novi. "People were confusing Libra and Calibra all the time," said Marcus. "In hindsight it's hard to blame them."[293]

Facebook's various financial initiatives — Novi (formerly Calibra), Facebook Pay and WhatsApp Pay — were consolidated in July 2020 into Facebook Financial (F2), with Marcus in charge. "We have a lot of commerce stuff going on across Facebook," he told Bloomberg. "It felt like it was the right thing to do to rationalize the strategy at a company level around all things payments."[294]

## Libra going forward

Morgan Beller, who originally started Facebook's blockchain initiative in 2017, said in June 2020: "We're trying to change the system, and there are a lot of people who are incentivized for the global financial system not to change."[6]

Maybe regulators were just a bunch of haters — or maybe Libra was a bad idea, done badly, by a badly-behaved company.

Libra was born in Bitcoin dreams — but none of those aspirations could ever have been realised, because they contradicted everything about how economics and consumer finance work in the real world.

The fallacy of Libra, and of cryptocurrency plans in general, is that the problem isn't that we need a new technology. We know how to move numbers on a computer. The problems with Libra were always going to be regulation — especially when the project came from Facebook.

Crypto dreams are tolerated when they're put forward by weird small-time nutters — but not when they're coming from a huge company with a continent-sized user base.

But, even though every single thing about Libra went wrong, Facebook doesn't take "no" or "never" for an answer. Work proceeds on the Novi wallet, the Libra blockchain software, and proposals for regulators — even if Facebook is still the only Association member putting in funding or engineering effort.

The Libra Association spent 2020 hiring executive staff with experience at large banks like HSBC and regulators such as FinCEN. The Association anticipates final regulatory permission to launch a Libra payment network some time in 2021. Or something called "Libra," at least.

Morgan Beller left Facebook in September 2020 and joined venture capital firm NFX as a General Partner,[295] focusing on early-stage investing. "Being part of Libra from the earliest days made me realize that I love that phase of a project — the sitting around and figuring out what we should do," she said.[296] That is: having big ideas is much more fun than delivering on them.

# Appendix:
# 2010–2013: The rise and fall of Facebook Credits

Libra wasn't Facebook's first foray into payment systems. In 2009, the company set up Facebook Credits, to cash in on pay-to-win games.

When Libra was announced in June 2019, Facebook told Barron's that "Facebook Credits was a completely closed system, and this is open and decentralized."[297] But it's an instructive example as Facebook's first attempt. The company didn't have run-ins with regulators — but they did try to gouge a captive audience of partners.

## Pay-to-win — hitting the gambling addicts

Pay-to-win games are common on phones. You can start playing for free — but the game gets harder and harder, and you eventually have to buy power-ups with real money to progress at all. "Free-to-pay" is the standard industry euphemism. Candy Crush is a famous recent example.

Pay-to-win games weren't new with smartphones. A decade ago, the games ran in Facebook — on your desktop PC's web browser, in Flash.

There was a lot of money in pay-to-win — Zynga, makers of Farmville and Mafia Wars, took in $597 million in 2010.[298] For comparison, Facebook's own revenue in 2010 was just under $2 billion.[299]

More than 90% of Zynga's revenue was users buying in-game coins, which they could use to buy power-ups. PayPal said that Zynga was its second-biggest merchant for 2009 — only beaten by eBay, PayPal's owner.[300]

Facebook saw what its platform was being used for, and just how much money its developers were taking in, and decided it wanted a piece of that.

# The genesis of Credits

Facebook started developing an in-app currency system in 2007, and ran a closed beta in December 2007.[301]

In November 2008, the company put a system of "credits" into the Facebook Gift Shop, where you could buy virtual gifts — pixels on a screen to amuse your friends with. Gifts that were previously $1 would now be 100 credits.[302]

"The new system means we can introduce a wider variety of gifts," Facebook explained, "allowing you greater freedom in expressing appreciation for your friends" — though they didn't explain how these credits would do this better than dollars had.

The system that was finally released as Facebook Credits was introduced for early testing in May 2009, with an official beta starting in February 2010.[303]

Rather than buy coins inside a game directly, Facebook wanted you to use Facebook Credits — ten Credits cost one US dollar, or about the same in several other currencies. You could buy Credits with a credit card or PayPal, or from the gift card rack in shops.

The idea of Credits was that an official currency for the whole platform would decrease payment friction, and so increase spending. Users were encouraged to buy large amounts of credits at a time — 50 credits cost $5, but 2,360 credits cost $200, an 18% discount.[304]

Developers could use the "credit_balance" interface to see how many Credits a user had[305] — and Facebook confirmed that developers could use this to identify the biggest Credit holders, and squeeze them for even more money.[306]

By February, the Credits beta was already going well — Facebook said that "early testing has shown that users paying with Facebook Credits are significantly more likely to complete a purchase than the average Facebook user."[303] By October 2010, there were 200 games using Facebook Credits[307] — including several of the most popular ones.

# Credits for everyone!

Credits had limitations. Developers couldn't charge a user in fractional Credits. They could only sell virtual goods. They couldn't sell anything related to alcohol or tobacco. They couldn't let users redeem Credits for actual currency, or exchange Credits with other users.[308]

When a developer wanted to cash in their Credits, Facebook took a 30% fee — the same swingeing fee that Apple charged in its App Store. Facebook Credits also had a chargeback mechanism for disgruntled users.

Facebook wanted Credits to become the *only* currency for apps running on the Facebook platform. Facebook had discussed with large developers in late 2009 their plans to make Credits mandatory,[309] and Mark Zuckerberg told Bloomberg TV in April 2010 that Facebook apps would have "one currency that people use."[310]

All apps were supposed to switch to Credits by the end of 2010 — but developers were dragging their feet. In January 2011, Facebook set a hard deadline of 1 July 2011 — all new apps would have to use Credits exclusively, and old apps would need to switch over.[311]

(My wife tells me that when she first set up an artist page on Facebook,[312] she'd get messages daily from Facebook telling her to buy Credits, so she could buy ads for her page. She got to the point of blocking messages from Facebook itself. Her artist page says it was created January 2013 — so Facebook was still pushing Credits as late as that.)

## Credits try to break out to the wider world

Facebook had wider ambitions for Credits — it wanted to turn Facebook Credits into a broader system for microtransactions and small purchases.[313] Facebook Payments Inc. was set up in December 2010 and registered in multiple US states.[314]

Warner Bros Digital Distribution experimented with renting movies for Credits. *The Dark Knight* was made available for rental for 30 Credits ($3) in early March 2011, and did well enough that five more movies were made available in late March.[315] A selection of movies could be rented for Credits through 2011.

You could use Credits as a currency on Facebook Deals, Facebook's four-month experiment in competing with group discount-buying startup Groupon. This was the first place you could use Facebook Credits to buy real things.[316]

## The death of Facebook Credits

Facebook updated its Android mobile app in October 2011 to include buying Facebook Credits — but the iPhone app couldn't use the system. This was because Apple *also* wanted to take its 30% cut, on top of Facebook's 30%. This was a serious problem as mobile became a more popular platform.[317]

Facebook deprecated Credits on 19 June 2012, in an announcement to developers: "Introducing subscriptions and local currency pricing."[318] Developers could now charge different prices in different countries — and offer subscriptions to games in local currencies. (A lesson the company didn't learn from for Libra.) Users' balances in Credits were converted back into the user's local currency.

Facebook Credits was finally removed on 13 September 2013.

So what killed Credits?

Facebook's user and developer base was becoming more international. Users were put off by figuring out weird currency conversion rates that changed daily. Game coins were way too expensive in poorer countries — there was no localised pricing.[319]

Credits gave developers a 5–10% increase in sales[320] — but this was eaten straight away by Facebook's 30% fee. A developer could only use alternative payment methods if they had an exclusive partnership with Facebook. Developers started actively seeking out other payment methods to avoid Facebook's fee.

Users had no reason to care about the Facebook Credits system. They'd buy Credits to put them into one or two of their favourite games — the Credits were just a way to play that game. Users didn't tend to keep Credits sitting around on their account.

Credits didn't work at all like money — users couldn't transfer Credits between themselves.

But Credits' biggest problem was that, by this time, desktop computer platforms were being replaced by mobile phones. Games were being developed to run as apps of their own, directly on the phones, not via Facebook — and the Flash versions of the games for Facebook didn't work on phones.

## What Facebook Credits means for Libra

It's not clear that Facebook tried all that hard to turn Facebook Credits into money people could use. Facebook Deals was the only place you could use Credits for physical goods — and that was only for a few months.

Turning Facebook Credits into a usable currency would have been a huge amount of work for Facebook, especially in fraud control and anti-money-laundering compliance — PayPal had enormous issues just turning a profit on small transactions in US dollars, without it all being eaten up fighting crooks.

The plus point for Libra was that Facebook didn't plan to keep all the value the system would generate — there was something in it for the other players in the system.

It's also not clear anyone with experience from Facebook Credits was even involved in Libra at any point — but relevant expertise is less welcome than you might think around blockchain dreams.

The old Facebook Credits web page now directs to something called Facebook Game Cards. The Facebook help page for Game Cards was last known to have worked in mid-2017.[321]

# Acknowledgements

The genesis of this book is a hot take on Libra that *Foreign Policy* commissioned a few days after Libra's launch in June 2019. James Palmer edited my quick ramblings into a hard-hitting article that enjoyed some popularity.[322] James might get a twitching red-pencil finger at points here, but I tried to keep him in mind as one of my target readers.

The loved one, Rose, puts up with me talking about cryptos all the time, and beta-reads everything I put out — vastly improving it. I figure buying the occasional gaming workstation is a pretty good deal.

I did try contacting the Libra Association and Facebook's Calibra/ Novi a number of times, and even sent them early drafts of the book — but my only input from Facebook was unofficial background from helpful people at Facebook and Calibra/Novi, who did their best to represent their company in a good light.

Thanks for questions, suggestions and editorial help go out to Falahuddin Arief, Tilman Bayer, Dave Birch (always good for 200-page PDFs with page references), Eric Biro, Oliver Blanthorn, Richard Gendal Brown, María José Calderón, Raúl Carrillo, Amy Castor, Katie Chan, Frances Coppola, Peter da Silva, Sonja Davidovic, Stephen Diehl, Ron Echeverri, Vincent Faidherbe, Caroline Ford, David Golumbia, Kevin Green, Aleksi Grym, Nigel Heffernan, Axel Johnston, Andrew Ketrow, John Kiff, J. P. Koning, Stephan Küffner, P. Majchrzak, Chris McKenna, Miriam Oudin, María Laura Patiño, Giles Payne, Colin Platt, Michael Reece Purson, Drew Robertson, David S. H. Rosenthal, Ed Salazar, John Smith, Tim Starling, Nicholas Weaver, Michael Westergaard (who came up with the title) — and many others who I can't name. This book is as good as it is because of all of you.

Particular thanks to Ariel Glenn, for cheerleading fabulously and relentlessly through the last few months of finishing up this "feel-good techno tragedy."

Sorry, you never asked so I never gave you the advice that while writing your first book is just failing at not writing a book the second book is actually a lengthy process of realizing that nothing you did on the first book actually works reliably.

— Elizabeth Sandifer

# About the author

David Gerard writes the cryptocurrency and blockchain news site *Attack of the 50 Foot Blockchain*, and is the author of the 2017 book *Attack of the 50 Foot Blockchain: Bitcoin, Blockchain, Ethereum & Smart Contracts.*

As well as being a crypto journalist, he works as a Unix system administrator, where his job includes keeping track of exciting new technologies, and advising against the bad ones. He has also been an award-winning music journalist (Western Australia Music Industry Awards, 1991), and has blogged about music at Rocknerd.co.uk since 2001.

Originally from Australia, he lives in east London with his spouse Arkady Rose and their daughter.

David remains a frequent, if occasionally annoyed, user of Facebook. You can see his official page at facebook.com/DavidGerard.author/

David's website is at davidgerard.co.uk/blockchain/

*Also by David Gerard*

# Attack of the 50 Foot Blockchain
## Bitcoin, Blockchain, Ethereum & Smart Contracts

An experimental new Internet-based form of money is created that anyone can generate at home; people build frightening firetrap computers full of video cards, putting out so much heat that one operator is hospitalised with heatstroke and brain damage.

A young physics student starts a revolutionary new marketplace immune to State coercion; he ends up ordering hits on people because they might threaten his great experiment, and is jailed for life without parole.

Fully automated contractual systems are proposed to make business and the law work better; the contracts people actually write are unregulated penny stock offerings whose fine print literally states that you are buying nothing of any value.

The biggest crowdfunding in history attracts $150 million on the promise that it will embody "the steadfast iron will of unstoppable code"; upon release it is immediately hacked, and $50 million is stolen.

How did we get here?

David Gerard covers the origins and history of Bitcoin to the present day, the other cryptocurrencies it spawned including Ethereum, the ICO craze and the 2017 crypto bubble, and the attempts to apply blockchains and smart contracts to business. Plus a case study on blockchains in the music industry.

Bitcoin and blockchains are not a technology story, but a psychology story.

Remember: if it sounds too good to be true, it almost certainly is.

"A sober riposte to all the upbeat forecasts about cryptocurrency" — New York Review of Books

"A very convincing takedown of the whole phenomenon" — BBC News

*Available from Amazon (Kindle or paperback) and all other ebook stores*

# Index

# Notes

1 Kevin Rooke. "Facebook Makes More Revenue Per User Than Netflix." The Spring, 24 March 2019. (archive)
2 Mike Isaac, Nathaniel Popper. "Facebook Plans Global Financial System Based on Cryptocurrency." New York Times, 18 June 2019.
3 David Marcus, Senate testimony, 16 July 2019.
4 Katie Paul, Anna Irrera. "Factbox: Facebook's cryptocurrency Libra and digital wallet Calibra." Reuters, 23 October 2019.
5 Facebook. "Coming in 2020: Calibra." Press release, 18 June 2019.
6 Kathryn Miles. "Visionaries: Morgan Beller." MIT Technology Review, June 2020.
7 Salvador Rodriguez. "Meet Morgan Beller, the 26-year-old woman behind Facebook's plan to make its own currency." CNBC, 20 July 2019.
8 Scott Gartenberg. "Beller '13: Undergrads Should Follow Passions." Cornell Daily Sun, 23 February 2014.
9 Connie Loizos. "Morgan Beller, co-creator of the Libra digital currency, just joined the venture firm NFX." TechCrunch, 22 September 2020.
10 Aimee Keane, Hannah Murphy, Kiran Stacey. "The state of Libra." Financial Times *Behind The Money* podcast, 24 October 2019.
11 "Full transcript: Facebook Messenger head David Marcus on Recode Decode." Recode, 19 June 2017.
12 Shannon Bond. "David Marcus, the man leading Facebook's charge into financial services." Financial Times, 22 June 2019.
13 John Donahoe. "David Marcus is PayPal's New President." PayPal blog, 29 March 2012. (archive)
14 Jordan Novet. "PayPal chief reams employees: Use our app or quit." VentureBeat, 11 February 2014.
15 Marcus' involvement in the early history of Bitcoin is largely drawn from: Nathaniel Popper. *Digital Gold: Bitcoin and the Inside Story of the Misfits and Millionaires Trying to Reinvent Money*. HarperCollins, 2015.
16 David Marcus. "Here's to an amazing team, and to new beginnings." LinkedIn, 9 June 2014.
17 Robert Hackett. "Libra Hangs in Limbo — and What's Next in the Digital Currency Race." Fortune, 19 December 2019.
18 Mark Zuckerberg. "Every year I take on a personal challenge to learn something new." Facebook, 4 January 2018.
19 Kurt Wagner. "Facebook is launching a new team dedicated to the blockchain. Messenger's David Marcus is going to run it." Recode, 8 May 2018.
20 David Marcus. "After nearly four unbelievably rewarding years leading Messenger, I have decided it was time for me to take on a new challenge." Facebook, 8 May 2018.
21 Alex Heath. "Facebook Plans to Create Its Own Cryptocurrency." Cheddar, 11 May 2018.
22 Sarah Frier, Julie Verhage. "Facebook Is Developing a Cryptocurrency for WhatsApp Transfers, Sources Say." Bloomberg 21 December 2018.
23 Suvashree Ghosh, Anto Antony. "WhatsApp Compliance Under India Review Before Payments Approval." Bloomberg, 14 August 2019.
24 Alex Heath, Tanaya Macheel. "Facebook's Blockchain Group Is on a Hiring Spree to Reinvent Money." Cheddar, 13 December 2018.

25  Tim Bradshaw, Martin Coulter, Hannah Murphy. "How Facebook raced to build Libra coin." Financial Times, 19 June 2019.

26  Nathaniel Popper, Mike Isaac. "Facebook and Telegram Are Hoping to Succeed Where Bitcoin Failed." New York Times, 28 February 2019.

27  Libra. "How to Become a Founding Member." Version dated 14 June 2019. (archive)

28  Elise Thomas. "The Ties That Bind Facebook's Libra." Wired, 10 July 2019.

29  Olga Kharif. "Libra Association Board Members Have Ties to Facebook." Bloomberg, 15 October 2019.

30  Danielle Abril. "Andreessen Horowitz: How Facebook's Libra Cryptocurrency Will Be Governed." Fortune, 19 June 2019.

31  Frank Chaparro, Ryan Todd. "Facebook acquired a trademark from a little-known tax company for its secret crypto project." The Block, 3 May 2019. (archive)

32  AnnaMaria Andriotis, Liz Hoffman, Peter Rudegeair, Jeff Horwitz. "Facebook Building Cryptocurrency-Based Payments System." Wall Street Journal, 2 May 2019.

33  AnnaMaria Andriotis, Peter Rudegeair, Liz Hoffman. "Facebook's New Cryptocurrency, Libra, Gets Big Backers." Wall Street Journal, 13 June 2019.

34  Frank Chaparro, Aislinn Keely. "Facebook's cryptocurrency partners revealed — we obtained the entire list of inaugural backers." The Block, 14 June 2019. (Archive of 30 June 2019.)

35  Hannah Murphy. "Facebook unveils new global digital coin called Libra." Financial Times, 18 June 2019.

36  Laura Noonan, Robert Armstrong, Nicholas Megaw, Stephen Morris. "Banks steer clear of Facebook's Libra project." Financial Times, 8 July 2019.

37  Laura Noonan, Patrick Temple-West. "Banks may cut ties with Facebook on Libra concerns, ING warns." Financial Times, 22 October 2019.

38  PayPal. "Why PayPal plans to be part of the Libra Association." Press release, 18 June 2019. (now deleted — archive copy)

39  Visa. "Visa announces intent to join the Libra Association." Press release, 18 June 2019. (archive)

40  Robert Armstrong. "The end of Libra?" Financial Times, 21 October 2019.

41  Nathaniel Popper. "Regulators Have Doubts About Facebook Cryptocurrency. So Do Its Partners." New York Times, 25 June 2019.

42  J. M. Keynes. A Tract on Monetary Reform. Chapter 4: "Alternative aims in monetray policy." p172. Macmillan, 1924.

43  Alex de Vries. "Bitcoin's Growing Energy Problem." Joule, 2(5), 801-805. doi:10.1016/j.joule.2018.04.016

44  The best available explanation of how the 1990s techno-libertarian subculture led to Bitcoin is The Politics of Bitcoin: Software as Right-Wing Extremism by David Golumbia (University of Minnesota Press, 2016).

45  @lopp. "On stage right now: people representing approximately 90% of the Bitcoin hashing power. Truly an historic moment." Twitter, 6 December 2015.

46  Larry Cermak. "The growth of the Lightning Network has been remarkable. But there's a catch." The Block, 15 January 2019. (archive)

47  Stephen Shankland. "PayPal president David Marcus: Bitcoin is good, NFC is bad." CNet, 10 December 2013.

48  @SquawkCNBC. "Does the creator of Libra own Bitcoin? 'I'm a big fan of bitcoin and what I see as digital gold,' says @DavidMarcus on #btc." Twitter, 16 October 2019.

49  Matt Levine. "Things Got Weird for Stablecoin Tether." Bloomberg, 26 April 2019.

50  "Frequently Asked Questions." Tether, archive of 20 March 2015. "You can fund your account with bitcoins and convert to Tethers to stabilize your bitcoins and without having to undertake KYC."

51  Richard Heffner. "Milton Friedman: Living Within Our Means." The Open Mind, Thirteen, 7 December 1975.

52  "Libra (Sept 24th to October 23)." Libra.org, archive of 25 October 2018.

53  "Libra: A New Global Currency." Libra.org, archive of 18 June 2019.

54  Frances Coppola. "Bananas Don't Make A Good Stablecoin." Forbes, 28 February 2019.

55  David Gerard. "Dentacoin — it's real and sincere, even if nobody cares." Blog post, 29 March 2019.

56  Libra Association Members. "An Introduction to Libra." Version dated 14 June 2019. (archive)

57  This metaphor — a riff on Pierre Trudeau's 1969 quote to the National Press Club on Canada's relationship with the US — is courtesy a Financial Times FT Alphaville comment I can't find again. Please get in touch with the original link for your credit!

58  Tim Bartz. "Facebook verzichtet bei Libra auf chinesische Währung." Der Spiegel, 20 September 2019.

59  Christian Catalini, Oliver Gratry, J. Mark Hou, Sunita Parasuraman, Nils Wernerfelt. "The Libra Reserve." Version dated 14 June 2019. (archive)

60  Elaine Ou. "I Tried Using Facebook's Libra Blockchain. It Didn't Work." Bloomberg Opinion, 20 June 2019.

61  Shehar Bano, Christian Catalini, George Danezis, Nick Doudchenko, Ben Maurer, Alberto Sonnino, Nils Wernerfelt. "Moving Toward Permissionless Consensus." Version dated 14 June 2019. (archive)

62  Paul A. McCulley. "Teton Reflections." Pimco blog, 7 September 2007.

63  Original quote: "Vamos a crear un sistema bancario reflejo usando tu moneda." Leaked audio in: David Gerard "Foreign Policy: Facebook's New Currency Has Big Claims and Bad Ideas — by me." Blog post, 24 June 2019.

64  Libra. "Commitment to Compliance and Consumer Protection." Version dated 14 June 2019. (archive)

65  Eric M. Jackson. The PayPal Wars: Battles with eBay, the Media, the Mafia, and the Rest of Planet Earth. Chapter 1: "The New Recruit." pp25-27. World Ahead Publishing, 2004. ISBN 1-936488590.

66  Peter Kropotkin. The Conquest of Bread. Chapter III part 1, p23. G. P. Putnam's Sons, 1906.

67  World Bank. Remittance Prices Worldwide. No. 34, June 2020.

68  e.g., Nick Statt. "Facebook's Calibra is a secret weapon for monetizing its new cryptocurrency." The Verge, 18 June 2019.

69  Ryan Browne. "Facebook exec says libra cryptocurrency won't spread 'like a social network'." CNBC, 5 November 2019.

70  Brendan Greeley. "Facebook's Libra will not help the unbanked." Financial Times FT Alphaville, 19 June 2019.

71  A. Demirgüç-Kunt, L. Klapper, D. Singer, S. Ansar, J. Hess. The Global Findex Database 2017: Measuring Financial Inclusion and the Fintech Revolution. World Bank Group, 2018. ISBN 978-1-4648-1268-2.

72  Carmen Nobel. "Mobile Banking for the Unbanked." Harvard Business School, 2011.

73  Peter Vanham. "Mobile money: Kenya good, India bad." Financial Times, 28 May 2012.

74  Lerato Mbele. "Why M-Pesa failed in South Africa." BBC News, 11 May 2016.

75   Leandro Medina, Friedrich Schneider. "Shadow Economies Around the World: What Did We Learn Over the Last 20 Years?" International Monetary Fund, January 2018.

76   Leonid Bershidsky. "The Upside to Facebook's Libra Disaster." Bloomberg Opinion, 15 October 2019.

77   James C. Scott. "Chapter 3: Authoritarian High Modernism." In *Seeing Like A State: How Certain Schemes to Improve the Human Condition Have Failed.* Yale University Press, 1998. ISBN 978-0-30007016-3.

78   Deirdre Fernandes. "Bitcoin doesn't gain much currency at MIT." Boston Globe, 27 September 2016.

79   "MIT Sloan Experts Series — Christian Catalini: Breaking Down the Libra Cryptocurrency." YouTube, 7 November 2019.

80   F. A. Hayek. *The Denationalisation Of Money.* Institute for Economic Affairs, 1976. ISBN 0 255 36239 0.

81   Ben Walsh. "Facebook's Libra Currency Will Be Tied, in Part, to the U.S. Dollar." Barron's, 23 September 2019.

82   Laura Shin. "A Libra Co-Creator on How Facebook Will Make Money From Calibra." Unchained (podcast), 5 November 2019.

83   Izabella Kaminska. "Zuckerbuck vs PayPal vs China." Financial Times FT Alphaville, 25 October 2019.

84   Denise Jia. "PBOC to Raise Reserve-Funds Ratio for Third-Party Payment Firms to 100%." Caixin Global, 30 June 2018.

85   "MFI balance sheets: Electronic money issued in the euro area." European Central Bank Statistical Data Warehouse, 17 February 2020.

86   Mitsutoshi Adachi, Matteo Cominetta, Christoph Kaufmann, Anton van der Kraaij. "A regulatory and financial stability perspective on global stablecoins." Macroprudential Bulletin, European Central Bank, 5 May 2020.

87   "GIC Private Limited (GIC)." Sovereign Wealth Fund Institute. Archive of 27 October 2020.

88   Frances Coppola. "Libra isn't just a cryptocurrency, it's a threat to national sovereignty." Wired, 16 October 2019.

89   "PBOC reins in funds of payment platforms." China Daily, 15 January 2019.

90   John Nugée. "What Libra means for money creation." OMFIF, 5 February 2020.

91   Izabella Kaminska. "Will fintechs sink or swim when floats are regulated?" Financial Times FT Alphaville, 7 January 2019.

92   *See* Paul J. Krugman. *The Return of Depression Economics and the Crisis of 2008.* Chapter 8: "Banking in the Shadows" and Chapter 9: "The Sum of All Fears." W. W. Norton, 2009. ISBN 978-0-393-07120-7.

93   "FINMA publishes 'stable coin' guidelines." FINMA, 11 September 2019.

94   Ben Walsh. "Facebook's Libra Currency Has an Interest-Rate Problem." Barron's, 6 September 2019.

95   Nicholas Comfort, Stephan Kahl. "German Banks Are Hoarding So Many Euros They Need More Vaults." Bloomberg, 31 January 2020.

96   Francesco Guarascio. "France, Germany blast Facebook's Libra, back public cryptocurrency." Reuters, 13 September 2019.

97   Michael Nienaber, Christian Kraemer. "Germany's Scholz: We cannot accept parallel currencies such as Facebook's Libra." Reuters, 17 September 2019.

98   @davidmarcus. "1/ About monetary sovereignty of Nations vs. Libra:" Twitter, 16 September 2019.

99   Bhavin Patel, Katie-Ann Wilson. "Libra and the global monetary system." OMFIF, 28 October 2019.

100 Ben Munster. "France vows to block Facebook's Libra in Europe." Decrypt, 12 September 2019

101 Raúl Carrillo. "Banking on Surveillance: The Libra black paper." Americans for Financial Reform Education Fund and Demand Progress Education Fund, 25 June 2020.

102 Shannon Greenwood, Andrew Perrin, Maeve Duggan. "Social Media Update 2016." Pew Research Center, 11 November 2016.

103 Federal Trade Commission. "FTC Imposes $5 Billion Penalty and Sweeping New Privacy Restrictions on Facebook." Press release, 24 July 2019.

104 Olivia Solon, Cyrus Farivar. "Leaked documents show Facebook leveraged user data to fight rivals and help friends." NBC News, 6 November 2019.

105 European Commission. "Mergers: Commission fines Facebook €110 million for providing misleading information about WhatsApp takeover." Press release, 18 May 2017.

106 Digital, Culture, Media and Sport Committee. "Disinformation and 'fake news': Final Report." House of Commons, 27 February 2019.

107 Emma Kent. "Oculus Quest 2 Facebook account merge turns some headsets into 'paperweights', affected users say." Eurogamer, 15 October 2020.

108 "A Single Way to Log Into Oculus and Unlock Social Features." Oculus blog, 18 August 2020.

109 Zeynep Tufecki. "Why Zuckerberg's 14-Year Apology Tour Hasn't Fixed Facebook." Wired, 6 April 2018.

110 Ben Munster. "With Libra, Facebook jumps on a long derailed bandwagon." Decrypt, 19 June 2019.

111 David Kirkpatrick. *The Facebook Effect*. Chapter 12: "$15 Billion." Simon & Schuster, 2010. ISBN 978-1-4391-0980-9.

112 Jeff Horwitz, Parmy Olson. "Facebook Unveils Cryptocurrency Libra in Bid to Reshape Finance." Wall Street Journal, 18 June 2019.

113 Pete Schroeder, Katie Paul. "U.S. Senate to grill Facebook over plans for Libra cryptocurrency." Reuters, 16 July 2019.

114 Tom Wilson, Huw Jones. "Facebook met UK officials three times before Libra announcement." 18 September 2019.

115 Laura Noonan, Hannah Murphy. "Facebook in talks with US regulator over digital currency." Financial Times, 2 June 2019.

116 "Facebook va créer sa monnaie : 'Nous allons demander des garanties', prévient Bruno Le Maire." Europe 1, 18 June 2019.

117 Caroline Binham, Chris Giles, David Keohane. "Facebook's Libra currency draws instant response from regulators." Financial Times, 18 June 2019.

118 Leigh Thomas, Myriam Rivet. "Consensus among G7 ministers to tackle Facebook's Libra: French chair." Reuters, 17 July 2019.

119 Leigh Thomas, Michael Nienaber. "G7 finance chiefs pour cold water on Facebook's digital coin plans." Reuters, 17 July 2019.

120 Francesco Canepa, Leigh Thomas. "Libra launch won't happen until regulators are happy: Coeure." Reuters, 18 July 2019.

121 Maxine Waters. "Waters Statement on Facebook's Cryptocurrency Announcement." Press release, US House Committee on Financial Services, 18 June 2019.

122 Elizabeth Dwoskin, Damian Paletta. "Facebook privately pitched its cryptocurrency plan last month to regulators. They were left even more scared." Washington Post, 16 July 2019.

123 Maxine Waters. "Committee Democrats Call on Facebook to Halt Cryptocurrency Plans." Press release, US House Committee on Financial Services, 2 July 2019.

124 Pete Schroeder, Trevor Hunnicutt. "Fed chief calls for Facebook to halt Libra project until concerns addressed." Reuters, 10 July 2019.

125 Jessica Smith. "Powell: Libra 'cannot go forward' without addressing serious concerns." Yahoo! Finance, 10 July 2019.

126 Matthew C. Klen. "Congress Is More Concerned About Facebook's Libra Currency Than Inflation." Barron's, 11 July 2019.

127 @realdonaldtrump. "....Similarly, Facebook Libra's 'virtual currency' will have little standing or dependability. If Facebook and other companies want to become a bank, they must seek a new Banking Charter and become subject to all Banking Regulations, just like other Banks, both National..." Twitter, 12 July 2019.

128 Dave Michaels, Lalita Clozel. "SEC Weighs Whether to Regulate Facebook's Libra." Wall Street Journal, 13 July 2019.

129 Aislinn Keely. "Video and Transcript of U.S. Treasury Secretary's Press Briefing on Cryptocurrencies." The Block, 15 July 2019.

130 Anna Irrera, Katie Paul. "Facebook's Libra coin likely to run a regulatory gauntlet." Reuters, 28 June 2019.

131 Katanga Johnson. "U.S. SEC chief says he has not met with Facebook since Libra announcement." Reuters, 16 July 2019.

132 Pete Schroeder, Ismail Shakil. "U.S. proposes barring big tech companies from offering financial services, digital currencies." Reuters, 14 July 2019.

133 Chris Hughes. "Facebook co-founder: Libra coin would shift power into the wrong hands." Financial Times, 21 June 2019.

134 Mark Carney. "Enable, empower, ensure: a new finance for the new economy." Bank of England, 20 June 2019.

135 Huw Jones, Leigh Thomas. "Facebook's Libra must be 'rock solid' before launch warns BoE's Carney." Reuters, 11 July 2019.

136 Huw Jones, David Milliken, Brenna Hughes Neghaiwi. "European watchdogs demand detail on Facebook's cryptocurrency." Reuters, 25 June 2019.

137 Caroline Binham. "UK regulator scrutinising Facebook's plan for digital currency." Financial Times, 25 June 2019.

138 Brendan Greeley. "Facebook's Libra currency is wake-up call for central banks." Financial Times, 21 October 2019.

139 "BIS Annual Economic Report." Bank for International Settlements, 23 June 2019.

140 Huw Jones, Tom Wilson. "Politicians need to move fast as Facebook & Co move into finance: BIS." Reuters, 23 June 2019.

141 Frank Tang. "Facebook's Libra forcing China to step up plans for its own cryptocurrency, says central bank official." South China Morning Post, 8 July 2019.

142 Mu Changchun. "Opinion: Facebook's Libra Needs Central Bank Supervision." Caixin Global, 9 July 2019.

143 David Marcus. "Libra, 2 weeks in." Facebook, 3 July 2019.

144 Jemima Kelly. "Facebook fights back against Libra criticism." Financial Times FT Alphaville, 5 July 2019.

145 Sheila Bair. "Why the Fed should oversee Facebook's Libra." Yahoo! Finance, 8 July 2019.

146 Alex Heath. "Facebook's Marcus Says Libra Association Will Be Independent 'by Launch'." The Information, 28 June 2019.

147 Scott Galloway. "The Arrogance and Genius of Libra Coin: Why Facebook's plans for a cryptocurrency are already dead in the water." Blog post, 25 June 2019.

148 Mike Crapo, Sherrod Brown. "Facebook letter." United States Senate Committee on Banking, Housing, and Urban Affairs, 9 May 2019.

149 "Facebook Digital Currency." C-SPAN, 16 July 2019. Quotes used in this chapter were checked against this video.

150 "Facebook Digital Currency." C-SPAN, 17 July 2019. Quotes used in this chapter were checked against this video.

151 Kiran Stacey, Hannah Murphy. "Facebook's cryptocurrency hopes hit a wall in Washington." Financial Times, 18 July 2019.

152 Josh Constine. "Facebook announces Libra cryptocurrency: All you need to know." TechCrunch, 18 June 2019.

153 Josh Constine. "We still don't know how much of Libra Facebook owns." TechCrunch, 3 July 2019.

154 David Marcus. "Testimony of David Marcus: Head of Calibra, Facebook." Senate Banking Committee, 15 July 2019.

155 Elizabeth Schulze. "Swiss group that's supposed to oversee privacy for Libra says it hasn't heard from Facebook at all." CNBC, 16 July 2019.

156 Brenna Hughes Neghaiwi. "Swiss watchdog expects details on Facebook's Libra by end of month." Reuters, 20 August 2019.

157 Greg Ip. "Facebook's Libra Could Give Dollar, Banks Some Welcome Competition." Wall Street Journal, 26 June 2019.

158 @Libra_. "By creating a de facto central bank, Libra could succeed where other cryptocurrencies fall short. More from @wsj:" Twitter, 16 July 2019. Archived by Maya Zehavi.

159 "Examining Facebook's Proposed Cryptocurrency and Its Impact on Consumers, Investors, and the American Financial System." US House Committee on Financial Services, 17 July 2019.

160 Chris Brummer. "Written Testimony of Chris Brummer: 99 Problems." 15 July 2019.

161 Katharina Pistor. "Written Statement of Proposed Testimony." 16 July 2019.

162 "Congress and Regulators Should Impose a Moratorium on Facebook's Libra." Public Citizen, 2 July 2019.

163 Robert Weissman. "Written Testimony of Robert Weissman: President, Public Citizen." 16 July 2019.

164 Gary Gensler. "Examining Facebook's Proposed Cryptocurrency and Its Impact on Consumers, Investors, and the American Financial System." 16 July 2019.

165 Meltem Demirors. "Written Testimony Of Meltem Demirors: Chief Strategy Officer CoinShares." 16 July 2019.

166 Libra. "The Libra Association." Version dated 23 July 2019. (archive)

167 Libra. "The Libra Association." Version dated 12 August 2019. (archive)

168 FINMA. "FINMA publishes 'stable coin' guidelines." Press release, 11 September 2019.

169 Thomas Fuster, Hansueli Schöchli. "Finma-Direktor Mark Branson: «Wenn ein Finanzplatz Ambitionen hat, muss er mit Aufmerksamkeit leben können»." Neue Zürcher Zeitung, 12 September 2019. "Ein Projekt mit einer derart globalen Dimension kann nur in internationaler Koordination und in Absprache mit anderen Aufsichts- und Regulierungsbehörden angegangen werden."

170 Angelika Gruber. "Switzerland's FINMA boss fears crypto's 'dark corners,' not Libra." Reuters, 1 October 2019.

171 Thomas Jordan. "Currencies, money and digital tokens." Swiss National Bank, 5 September 2019.

172 The Federal Council. "Federal Council informed of current status of stablecoin debate." Press release, 16 October 2019.

173 Lydia Beyoud, Aoife White. "Facebook's Libra Currency Gets European Union Antitrust Scrutiny." Bloomberg, 20 August 2019.

174 Yves Mersch. "Money and private currencies: reflections on Libra." European Central Bank, 2 September 2019.

175 @gregory_raymond. "Selon mes infos, les autorités FR n'ont pas reçu de demande d'agrément de @Libra_ (indisp. pour opérer dans l'UE). À leur connaissance, même chose ailleurs dans l'UE : 'Face aux risques identifiés, Facebook n'a pour l'instant apporté aucune réponse aux autorités publiques'." Twitter, 12 September 2019.

176 Francesco Guarascio. "Spooked by Libra, EU pledges to regulate digital currencies." Reuters, 8 October 2019.

177 Sam Fleming, Mehreen Khan. "Facebook questioned by Brussels over Libra risks." Financial Times, 6 October 2019.

178 Mark Carney. "The Growing Challenges for Monetary Policy in the current International Monetary and Financial System." Jackson Hole Symposium, 23 August 2019.

179 Claire Jones. "The problems of the global monetary order go deeper than Trump." Financial Times FT Alphaville, 27 August 2019.

180 Bowdeya Tweh, Peter Rudegeair. "Facebook CEO to Testify at House Panel About Libra." Wall Street Journal, 9 October 2019.

181 Katanga Johnson. "U.S. securities chief 'not prepared' to say if Facebook's Libra a security." Reuters, 24 September 2019.

182 Brenna Hughes Neghaiwi. "Swiss-based Libra will have to meet tough U.S. standards: U.S. Treasury." Reuters, 10 September 2019.

183 Hugo Miller. "Facebook's Libra Will Be Under U.S. Money-Laundering Scrutiny." Bloomberg, 10 September 2019.

184 Michael Roddan. "Facebook faces inquiry on Libra currency." The Australian, 6 November 2019.

185 Stefania Palma. "Singapore joins calls for global approach to Facebook's Libra." Financial Times, 19 September 2019.

186 Madhumita Murgia. "Facebook data pledges for digital currency questioned." Financial Times, 19 June 2019.

187 Besnik Dervishi, Angelene Falk, Daniel Therrien, Marguerite Ouedraogo Bonane, Giovanni Buttarelli, Elizabeth Denham, Rohit Chopra. "Joint statement on global privacy expectations of the Libra network." 5 August 2019.

188 "It doesn't matter if Facebook's Libra fails: Analyst." (video) CNBC, 17 July 2019.

189 Michelle Davis. "Facebook's Libra Is 'Neat Idea That'll Never Happen,' Dimon Says." Bloomberg, 18 October 2019.

190 Hannah Murphy, Shannon Bond. "Facebook's Libra backers look to distance themselves from project." Financial Times, 23 August 2019.

191 Hannah Murphy, Kiran Stacey. "PayPal on the verge of quitting Facebook's Libra project." Financial Times, 3 October 2019.

192 AnnaMaria Andriotis, Peter Rudegeair. "Visa, Mastercard, Others Reconsider Involvement in Facebook's Libra Network." Wall Street Journal, 1 October 2019.

193 @davidmarcus. "The part of this article suggesting we weren't on top of, or didn't share detailed information about how to secure Libra and protect the network against illegal activity is categorically untrue; (worth calling BS)." Twitter, 2 October 2019.

194 Peter Rudegeair. "PayPal Drops Out of Facebook's Libra Payments Network." Wall Street Journal, 4 October 2019.

195 Sherrod Brown. "Brown, Schatz Warn Payments Providers of Risks with Libra Association." Press release, 8 October 2019.

196 Laurence Dodds. "Exodus from Facebook's Libra digital currency as Visa, Mastercard and other backers quit." Daily Telegraph, 11 October 2019.

197 Robert Armstrong. "Mastercard chief speaks out against nationalism and Facebook." Financial Times, 3 February 2020.
198 Hannah Murphy, Kiran Stacey. "Where it all went wrong for Facebook's Libra." Financial Times, 15 October 2019.
199 Chris Giles, Kiran Stacey, Hannah Murphy. "Global regulators put pressure on Libra with enhanced scrutiny." Financial Times, 13 October 2019.
200 United States Senate Committee on Banking, Housing, and Urban Affairs. "Brown Statement On Payment Providers Declining To Join Facebook's Libra Association." Press release, 11 October 2019.
201 Lauren Feiner. "Treasury Secretary Mnuchin says libra backers dropped out because the project is 'not ready' to meet regulatory standards." CNBC, 14 October 2019.
202 Michael Nienaber. "Withdrawal of companies from Libra project is a good sign: Scholz." Reuters, 15 October 2019.
203 Joe Light, Olivia Carville. "Libra Loses a Quarter of Its Members as Booking Holdings Exits." Bloomberg, 14 October 2019.
204 Alice Hancock. "Priceline owner becomes latest to drop Facebook's Libra." Financial Times, 14 October 2019.
205 @davidmarcus. "I would caution against reading the fate of Libra into this update. Of course, it's not great news in the short term, but in a way it's liberating. Stay tuned for more very soon. Change of this magnitude is hard. You know you're on to something when so much pressure builds up." Twitter, 11 October 2019.
206 Michelle Price. "Facebook executive confident Libra will win enough financial backers." Reuters, 16 October 2019.
207 Corinne Reichert, Andrew Morse. "Facebook's Libra cryptocurrency loses support of five founding members." CNet, 14 October 2019.
208 Bruno Le Maire. "Facebook's Libra is a threat to national sovereignty." Financial Times, 17 October 2019.
209 "Interview with Bloomberg." European Central Bank, 17 October 2019.
210 Tom Wilson. "'Stablecoins' could hinder efforts to stamp out money laundering: global watchdog." Reuters, 18 October 2019.
211 Yanis Varoufakis. "The IMF Should Take Over Libra." Project Syndicate, 18 October 2019.
212 Randal K. Quarles. "To G20 Finance Ministers and Central Bank Governors." Financial Stability Board, 13 October 2019.
213 Lael Brainard. "Digital Currencies, Stablecoins, and the Evolving Payments Landscape." The Future of Money in the Digital Age, 16 October 2019.
214 Mehreen Khan, Sam Fleming, Caroline Binham. "Central banks to grill Facebook over Libra." Financial Times, 15 September 2019.
215 Patrick Jenkins. "Life after Libra: how regulators could fuel rise of digital currency." Financial Times, 21 October 2019.
216 G7 Working Group on Stablecoins. "Investigating the impact of global stablecoins." Committee on Payments and Market Infrastructures, Bank for International Settlements, 17 October 2019.
217 Libra Association. "Libra Association Fact Sheet: Libra Meetings on October 14, 2019." Press release, 14 October 2019.
218 Kiran Stacey, Hannah Murphy. "Zuckerberg warns blocking Libra will be boon to China tech." Financial Times, 23 October 2019.
219 Dave Lee. "Facebook's partners yet to commit money to Libra." BBC News, 23 October 2019.
220 Kiran Stacey, Hannah Murphy. "Facebook admits digital currency doubts as regulatory hurdles loom." Financial Times, 14 October 2019.

221 Cecilia Kang, Nathaniel Popper. "Facebook Lays On the Charm for Its Libra Cryptocurrency Plan." New York Times, 21 October 2019.
222 US House Committee on Financial Services. "Facebook CEO to Testify Before Financial Services Committee." Press release, 9 October 2019.
223 Emily Birnbaum, Silvan Lane. "Live coverage: Zuckerberg testifies before House on Facebook's Libra project." The Hill, 23 October 2019.
224 "Facebook CEO Testimony Before House Financial Services Committee." C-SPAN, 23 October 2019.
225 "Mark Zuckerberg Testimony Transcript: Zuckerberg Testifies on Facebook Cryptocurrency Libra." Rev.com (third-party transcript), 24 October 2019. This transcript was the main source for this chapter, with quotes checked against the C-SPAN video.
226 "Congressman Jesús 'Chuy' García Introduces Bill to Keep Big Tech Companies Out of Financial Sector." Press release, 23 October 2019.
227 "FTAV Person of Interest 2019: The Longlist." Financial Times, 23 December 2019.
228 "Facebook Q3 2019 Earnings." Facebook Investor Relations, 30 October 2019.
229 Martine Paris. "Full speed ahead for Calibra, says Facebook's Kevin Weil." Modern Consensus, 1 November 2019.
230 Paul Sawers. "Facebook comparing Libra to the open internet rings hollow." VentureBeat, 5 November 2019.
231 "Articles of Association of Libra Association." 20 November 2019.
232 "Articles of Association of Libra Association." 31 July 2019.
233 Michael Engle. "Steering Committee now governs Libra technical development." Libra Association, 16 January 2020.
234 Nikhilesh De. "Vodafone Is the Latest Big Company to Quit Facebook-Founded Libra Association." CoinDesk, 21 January 2020.
235 Shopify. "Shopify joins Libra Association." Press release, 21 February 2020.
236 Josh Constine. "Facebook's Libra Association adds crypto prime broker Tagomi." TechCrunch, 26 February 2020.
237 Pierre Ferrari. "Heifer International Joins the Libra Association." Blog post, 20 April 2020.
238 Guillaume Pousaz. "Checkout.com joins the Libra association." Blog post, 28 April 2020.
239 Libra Association. "The Libra Association announces new members." Press release, 14 May 2020.
240 Libra Association. "The Libra Association welcomes Blockchain Capital as its newest member." Press release, 18 September 2020.
241 International Organization of Securities Commissions. "Statement on IOSCO study of emerging global stablecoin proposals." Press release, 5 November 2019.
242 "Rep. Sylvia Garcia and Rep. Lance Gooden Introduce the Managed Stablecoins are Securities Act of 2019." Press release, 21 November 2019.
243 The European Council. "Joint statement by the Council and the Commission on 'stablecoins.'" Press release, 5 December 2019.
244 "Ueli Maurer zieht Bilanz: «Die Schweiz redet mit allen»." SRF News, 27 December 2019.
245 Bhavin Patel, Pierre Ortlieb. "Digital Currencies: A question of trust." OMFIF, 5 February 2020.
246 Alex Hickey. "Facebook Introduces Facebook Pay." Morning Brew, 12 November 2019.
247 Deborah Liu. "Simplifying Payments with Facebook Pay." Facebook, 12 November 2019.

248  "Send Money to Friends in Messenger." Facebook, 17 March 2015.
249  Josh Constine. "Facebook Introduces Free Friend-To-Friend Payments Through Messages." TechCrunch, 17 March 2015.
250  Ingrid Lunden. "Facebook is discontinuing P2P payments in Messenger in the UK and France on June 15." TechCrunch, 16 April 2019.
251  Mark Zuckerberg. "Every new year of the last decade I set a personal challenge." Facebook, 9 January 2020.
252  "Implications for central banks of the development of electronic money." Bank for International Settlements, 1 October 1996.
253  J. P. Koning. "Why the Fed is more likely to adopt bitcoin technology than kill it off." Moneyness (blog), 14 April 2013.
254  J. P. Koning. "Fedcoin." Moneyness (blog), 19 October 2014.
255  The phrase "central bank digital currency" seems to have been coined by Richard Gendal Brown of enterprise blockchain company R3, in his blog post "A Central Bank "cryptocurrency"? An interesting idea, but maybe not for the reason we think," 5 March 2015. The initialism "CBDC" was first sighted in a speech by Ben Broadbent of the Bank of England, "Central banks and digital currencies," 2 March 2016.
256  Claire Jones. "Central bank plans to create digital currencies receive backing." Financial Times, 30 June 2019.
257  Aleksi Grym. "Lessons learned from the world's first CBDC." BoF Economics Review 8/2020, 15 September 2020.
258  Jennifer Sondag, Nathan Gill. "Ecuador Turning to Virtual Currency After Oil Loans." Bloomberg, 11 August 2014.
259  Everett Rosenfeld. "Ecuador becomes the first country to roll out its own digital cash." CNBC, 9 February 2015.
260  Evelyn Tapia. "Cinco cambios para impulsar el dinero móvil." El Comercio, 18 December 2017.
261  "71% de cuentas de dinero electrónico, sin uso en Ecuador." El Universo, 3 December 2017.
262  María Laura Patiño. "El dinero electrónico, una apuesta peligrosa." El Universo, 1 June 2016.
263  "Juan Pablo Guerra: Dinero electrónico es un medio de pago, no moneda." El Universo, 3 December 2017.
264  "Ecuador: Cuentas de dinero electrónico dejarán de funcionar el 31 de marzo." El Universal, 26 March 2018.
265  Mario Bergara, Jorge Ponce. "Central Bank Digital Currency: The Uruguayan e-Peso case." In *Do We Need Central Bank Digital Currency? Economics, Technology and Institutions.* ed. Ernest Gnan, Donato Masciandaro. SUERF, 2018.
266  "Project Sand Dollar: A Bahamas Payments System Modernisation Initiative." Central Bank of the Bahamas, 24 December 2019.
267  Jim Wyss. "Bahamas Plans E-Currency to Connect Far-Flung Island Beaches." Bloomberg, 15 September 2020.
268  "ECCB Digital EC Currency Pilot: Frequently Asked Questions." Eastern Caribbean Central Bank.
269  Mu Changchun, Di Gang, Lu Yuan, Qian Youcai, Qing Su De'. "央行数字货币研究所谈区块链技术的发展与管理." ("The Central Bank Digital Currency Research Institute talks about the development and management of blockchain technology.") Sina Technology, 21 February 2020.
270  Fan Yifei. "关于数字人民币 M0 定位的政策含义分析" ("Analysis on the Policy Implications of Digital RMB M0 Positioning.") China Financial News Network, 14

September 2019.

271 Frank Tang. "China has 'no timetable' for launch of its digital currency, says central bank governor." South China Morning Post, 24 September 2019.

272 "Interview with PBC Governor Yi Gang by Financial News and China Finance on Key Issues During 'Two Sessions'." People's Bank of China, 30 May 2020.

273 Reserve Bank of Australia. "Payments System Board Update: August 2020 Meeting." Press release, 21 August 2020.

274 @aleksigrym. "You hit the nail on the head. There is no innovation whatsoever. They have literally invented nothing. Libra is possibly the least innovative project to ever come out of Silicon Valley." Twitter, 4 March 2020.

275 Andrea Shalal. "Facebook open to currency-pegged stablecoins for Libra project." Reuters, 20 October 2019.

276 Hannah Murphy. "Shopify joins Facebook's Libra currency association." Financial Times, 21 February 2020.

277 Joe Light, Benjamin Bain, Olga Kharif. "Facebook Weighs Libra Revamp to Address Regulatory Concerns." Bloomberg, 3 March 2020.

278 Alex Heath. "Facebook Revamps Libra Plans, Bowing to Regulators." The Information, 3 March 2020.

279 Libra Association. "Libra Association applies for payment system license from FINMA." Press release, 16 April 2020.

280 FINMA. "Libra Association: FINMA licensing process initiated." Press release, 16 April 2020.

281 Libra Association. "White Paper v2.0." Archive of 16 April 2020.

282 "Congresswoman Sylvia Garcia's Response to Facebook Libra's Announcement about its Restructuring." Press release, 15 April 2020.

283 Kiran Stacey, Hannah Murphy. "How Facebook's Libra went from world changer to just another PayPal." Financial Times, 17 April 2020.

284 "FATF Report to G20 on So-called Stablecoins." Financial Action Task Force, 7 July 2020.

285 Andrew Bailey. "Reinventing the wheel (with more automation)." BIS, 3 September 2020.

286 Jorge Valero. "LEAK: EU to create 'superbody' of watchdogs to oversee digital currencies." Euractiv, 10 September 2020.

287 "Addressing the regulatory, supervisory and oversight challenges raised by 'global stablecoin' arrangements: Consultative document." Financial Stability Board, 14 April 2020.

288 "Regulation, Supervision and Oversight of 'Global Stablecoin' Arrangements." Financial Stability Board, 13 October 2020.

289 "Enhancing Cross-border Payments: Stage 3 roadmap." Financial Stability Board, 13 October 2020.

290 Carolina Mandl, Marcela Ayres. "Communication collapse: Inside Facebook's tussle with Brazil's central bank." Reuters, 16 July 2020.

291 Mario Sergio Lima, Kurt Wagner. "Brazilian Authorities Suspend WhatsApp Payments." Bloomberg, 23 June 2020.

292 Marcela Ayres, Jamie McGeever, Gabriela Mello, Chris Reese, Tom Brown. "Brazil central bank chief says WhatsApp payments service faces further review." Reuters, 2 July 2020.

293 Kurt Wagner. "Facebook Renames Blockchain Division After Libra Confusion." Bloomberg, 26 May 2020.

294 Kurt Wagner. "Facebook Financial Formed to Pursue Company's Payments Plans." Bloomberg, 10 August 2020.

295 Melia Russell. "Morgan Beller, the 27-year-old VC who led Facebook's Libra project, is the next Bill Gurley, her new boss says." Business Insider, 22 September 2020.

296 "Announcing our new General Partner, Morgan Beller." NFX blog, 22 September 2020.

297 Ben Walsh. "What Facebook's Cryptocurrency Libra Is Really About." Barron's, 21 June 2019.

298 " Zynga Revenue 2009-2019 | ZNGA." MacroTrends.

299 "Facebook Revenue 2009-2019 | FB." MacroTrends.

300 Chris Morrison. "Zynga Was PayPal's Second-Largest Merchant in 2009." AdWeek, 18 March 2010. (archive)

301 Justin Smith. "Facebook beta testing Platform payment system." Inside Facebook, 18 December 2007. (archive)

302 Justin Smith. "Facebook Exchanges Dollars for Virtual Credits, Eyes Expanding Virtual Gifts Revenues." Inside Facebook, 2 November 2008. (archive)

303 Deborah Liu. "Expanding Our Commitment to Facebook Credits." Facebook Developer Blog, 25 February 2010. (archive)

304 "Facebook scraps its own Credits currency for apps." BBC News, 20 June 2012.

305 "Facebook Credits API." Facebook Developers. (archive)

306 Josh Constine. "The Facebook Credits GetBalance API Helps Developers Dynamically Price Virtual Goods." Inside Facebook, 4 March 2011. (archive)

307 George Lee. "Expanding Facebook Credits." Facebook Developer Blog, 13 October 2010.

308 "Facebook Credits Terms." Facebook, 25 February 2010. (archive)

309 Eric Eldon. "Facebook Talking to Developers About New Plans for Its Virtual Currency." Inside Facebook, 25 November 2009. (archive)

310 Douglas MacMillan. "Zynga and Facebook. It's Complicated." Bloomberg Businessweek, 22 April 2010. (archive)

311 Eric Eldon. "Facebook Sets July, 1, 2011 Deadline to Make Credits Sole Canvas Game Payment Option." AdWeek, 24 January 2011. (archive)

312 Arkadian Dreams, facebook.com/arkadiandreams — buy a T-shirt!

313 Miguel Helft. "Facebook Hopes Credits Make Dollars." New York Times, 22 September 2010.

314 Owen Thomas. "Watch out, PayPal: Facebook gets serious about payments." VentureBeat, 21 March 2011.

315 Josh Constine. "Traction for The Dark Knight Leads Warner Bros to Rent More Films Via Facebook." AdWeek, 28 March 2011. (archive)

316 Miguel Helft. "Facebook Is Latest Rival to Groupon and LivingSocial." New York Times, 25 April 2011.

317 Matt Rosoff. "Facebook Totally Caved To Apple On Its New Mobile Platform." Business Insider, 10 October 2011. (archive)

318 Prashant Fuloria. "Introducing subscriptions and local currency pricing." Facebook Developer Blog, 19 June 2012.

319 Josh Constine. "Facebook Sunsets Credits, Transitions To Local Currencies To Boost International Payments." TechCrunch, 13 September 2013.

320 Eric Eldon. "Facebook's Increasing Focus on Credits Prompts Developer Speculation." Inside Facebook, 18 February 2010. (archive)

321 "Facebook Game Payments." Facebook Help Center. (Archive of 4 June 2017.)

322 David Gerard. "Facebook's New Currency Has Big Claims and Bad Ideas." Foreign Policy, 24 June 2019.

Printed in Great Britain
by Amazon